INNER
Excellence
at
Work

Other Books By Carol Orsborn

*The Art of Resilience: 100 Paths to Wisdom and Strength in an
    Uncertain World*. New York: Three Rivers Press, 1997.
Speak the Language of Healing: A New Approach to Breast Cancer.
    Emeryville, Calif.: Conari, 1999. (With Susan Kuner,
    Linda Quigley, and Karen Stroup.)
Enough Is Enough: Simple Solutions for Complex People. New
    York: Putnam, 1986. Order through Web site:
    www.innerexcellence.com.
*How Would Confucius Ask for a Raise: One Hundred Enlightened
    Solutions for Tough Business Problems*. New York: Avon
    Books, 1994.
    Order through Web site: www.innerexcellence.com.
Return From Exile: One Woman's Journey Back to Judaism. New
    York: Continuum, 1998.
*Solved by Sunset: The Right-Brain Way to Resolve Whatever's
    Bothering You in One Day or Less*. New York: Three Rivers
    Press, 1995.

INNER
Excellence
at
Work

THE PATH TO MEANING, SPIRIT, AND SUCCESS

Carol M. Orsborn

AMACOM
American Management Association

New York • Atlanta • Boston • Chicago • Kansas City • San Francisco • Washington, D.C.
Brussels • Mexico City • Tokyo • Toronto

This publication is designed to provide accurate and authoritative information in regard to the subject matter covered. It is sold with the understanding that the publisher is not engaged in rendering legal, accounting, or other professional service. If legal advice or other expert assistance is required, the services of a competent professional person should be sought.

Library of Congress Cataloging-in-Publication Data

Orsborn, Carol M.
   Inner excellence at work : the path to meaning, spirit, and success / Carol M. Orsborn.
      p.   cm.
   Originally published: San Rafael, Calif. : New World Library, c1992.
   Includes index.
   ISBN 0-8144-7041-6
   1. Success in business.   2. Creative ability in business.
3. Excellence.   4. Self-actualization (Psychology)   5. Self-realization.   6. Stress management.   I. Title.
HF5386.069   2000   99-29738
650.1--dc21   CIP

Printing number

10   9   8   7   6   5   4   3   2   1

To my partner in business and in life, Dan Orsborn
And to our beloved children, Grant and Jody

AUTHOR'S NOTE

Former and current clients of The Orsborn Company Public Relations have contributed case histories and anecdotal support for the principles shared in this book. When requested, I have honored their desire for anonymity by changing personal and company names and fictionalizing details.

Contents

Part One
The Challenge

*Personal values and quality of life considerations
need not conflict with ambition and success. In fact,
it is from these very qualities that your greatest
experience of success will grow.*

*In order to find a lasting experience of success in
unstable times, you must learn to tap into new, life-
driven sources of inspiration, creativity, and vitality.*

The unrest you are experiencing is not individual psychological difficulty, but rather part of a wider spiritual awakening.

Part Two
The Seven Principles of
Inner Excellence

Preface

Finding Meaning and Success
in a Changing World

*H*ow much of your ambition is fueled by inspiration, how much by fear?

Why is it that you have achieved so much and still feel something's missing?

What can you do when you bring your best to your work, and it isn't enough?

Most of us stop to ask ourselves questions like these at some point during our worklives. In search of answers, we buy books and take courses on how to prioritize our time better, improve our business and communication skills, do everything within our power to work harder, smarter, and tougher than the competition.

And still, the questions persist. Why? Because these issues are not a matter of strategy or manipulation, nor of effort, willpower, or brains. Beneath your yearning is the unabated desire for a relationship to the universe that makes sense of your life. It is not something wrong about you that yearns for meaning in your worklife. In fact, your restlessness and dissatisfaction are vital signs that you are on the threshhold of a new relationship to success that will bring you the fulfillment for which you yearn.

When I first formulated the Seven Principles of Inner Excellence nearly a decade ago, I knew that getting unhinged from the prevailing wisdom of the day was no small feat. Then, as now, there are forces at play in the contemporary workplace that encourage us to sleepwalk through unsatisfying careers and lives. In fact, as destructive as the prevailing work ethic was ten years ago, today's work culture has taken it to new extremes. We live in a workworld gone mad. Desperation masquerades as ambition. Greed and vanity are equated with success. In the contemporary workplace, people who try to play by the rules find themselves churned up by ever-growing machines that run over everything in their paths on the way to achieving corporate or institutional goals. Change and instability have become the norm.

Against this backdrop, I have come to realize the growing relevence of the principles I first formulated a decade ago. Over the years, I have heard from many readers who found in these pages the path to meaningful success — regardless of the circumstances with which they were faced. Some have read and reread this book many times, for it rouses people from old, self-destructive beliefs into the fresh air of expanded choices and opportunities. Today, more than ever, we need support in dealing with the fear that arises when we commit to taking sufficient time to tend our physical, spiritual, and emotional health. We need courage to deal with unruly bosses, clients, and workplaces. And not just once, but on an on-going basis, we need support as we traverse the challenges of the unknown. We don't have to be victims of uncertainty. We can, instead, allow ourselves to be initiated by change into a richer life.

As the decade has unfolded, I have had many opportunities to put my principles to the test. When I first wrote *Inner Excellence,* I imagined that I would continue to contentedly run our public relations agency in San Francisco, our guinea pig for these principles, forever. But as you undoubtedly know, nothing stays the same for long. A few years after the publication of this book, Dan, my husband and partner in the business, led our family on a new adventure, opening a home office for our firm in Nashville, Tennessee. Moving to "Music City" was the fulfillment of a lifelong dream. As fate would have it, we underestimated what it would take to keep San Francisco running in our periodic absences as well as what it would take to establish our business in a new community. However, by practicing the principles in this book, we managed to hold our center through the chaos.

We were not independently wealthy. We did not make this transition enjoying the comforts of uninterrupted salaries and income flow. What we did have was the passion to live out the Seven Principles of Inner Excellence no matter what—and the faith to see it through.

As the fog lifts, you will find us at last happily transplanted to our new city and life, operating a small and highly productive public relations agency flexible enough to encompass Dan's entry into the world of artist management as well as my completion of a graduate degree in religion at Vanderbilt University's outstanding divinity school, two long-held dreams that our relocation to Nashville made possible.

Through our challenges and disappointments, we have learned to be even less afraid of the dark places. This is a lesson mastered just in the nick of time, as in 1997, I was diagnosed and treated for breast cancer. It is a source of joy to me that the principles I formulated some time ago held true for me and my family under the greatest of challenges.

However, no writer revisiting her work ten years later could possibly resist making some changes. For starters, I have many new stories illustrating the principles to share with you. For those of you who have asked for more, here is the updated and expanded version of *Inner Excellence.*

As a result of my religious studies, you will also discover a greater emphasis on the importance of community in my writing. While self-realization remains a key component of the fully-lived life, I now realize that our ultimate responsibility and joy come out of our willingness to contribute to the greater good.

Another addition is the conscious embrace of paradox throughout the book. Before my theological training, I believed that a system of principles should be seamless and unconflicted. Taking inspiration from the prophets of the Hebrew Scriptures, I prefer now to wrestle publicly with discrepancies and gaps. There are times in our lives for peace and certainty; and there are times for us to shiver in awe in the shadow of mystery.

One of my key struggles has been whether to update my references to "the universe" with the word I now prefer to use for the divine mystery: "God." When I first wrote *Inner Excellence,* I used the less confrontive term "universe" because so many of us had lost faith in traditional religious conceptions of the divine. As I made my way through divinity school, I struggled with many of these conceptions one by one, reclaiming—in the end— the personal relationship with God my Jewish upbringing had promised. (I tell the tale of my journey in *Return From Exile: One Woman's Journey Back to Judaism,* Continuum Publishing, 1998.) My God is not just the universe, but the creator of the universe: beyond the grasp of my imagination, but as real to me as life itself. In the spirit of paradox, however, despite my own homecoming, I am reluctant to refer to the divine exclusively as God in the context of a business book to be read by people of many faiths. In this new edition of the book, I have decided to continue to meet the challenge of finding language that embraces diversity, without trivializing or generalizing the divine beyond recognition. I am hopeful that I have succeeded and that the words I choose to use in this version can serve as portals, rather than walls, to the divine.

When I first wrote *Inner Excellence,* I felt like I was often alone on my journey through the workplace. Faithful readers, even now, at the beginning of a new millennium, we are among the minority. But because of each other, we now know that we are not alone. Today, my book and principles have been embraced as part of the vibrant and growing spirituality and business movement. I am proud of what I wrote ten years ago and the role I have played in the popularization of these concepts. And I am grateful to you, my fellow travellers, for making this return trip possible!

ACKNOWLEDGMENTS

Nearly ten years ago, I had this crazy idea that there was some connection between spirituality and success in our worklives. When I would share my ideas with most people, they'd laugh at me: "You've got to be kidding. What does spirituality have to do with business?" But early on, I had the good fortune to connect with a few special people who decided to help me take my ideas public. Even then, I called them visionaries. With great appreciation, I thank my agent and friend Patti Breitman, editor Leslie Keenan, and marketing guru Munro Magruder of New World Library for helping me bring these principles to life.

A decade later, a new visionary has entered my world: Ellen Kadin, senior acquisitions editor at AMACOM Books. Ellen has given me that rarest of gifts: the opportunity to revisit the pages of my book and bring to them the advantages of another decade of life's experiences. As part of the American Management Association, Ellen and the people at AMACOM Books are taking these principles right into the heart of the mainstream business community. I am proud to be a part of this groundbreaking enterprise.

Finally, in gratitude for his courage, I acknowledge Dan Orsborn for joining me in turning our company and life into a living laboratory in which to test the practical application of alternative philosophies in a mainstream business environment. To paraphrase Helen Keller: "Life is an adventure or it is nothing." Dan, our life together is really something!

Part One

❦

The Challenge

Chapter One

The Discovery of Inner Excellence

*F*or years, I suffered the recurring nightmare that I was dancing on a stage in front of a packed audience—and had forgotten the steps. Little did I know that one spring day, a little over ten years ago, I was to suffer—in real life—as terrible a fate. On that balmy day, I was presenting a speech before an audience of my peers—nearly one thousand businesspeople who had flocked to an auditorium in a big U.S. city to hear my ideas about ambition and success.

The speech was not new. I had presented it an average of twice a month to audiences throughout the country ever since word of the organization I founded broke prominently in the *New York Times*. We called ourselves Overachievers Anonymous, the perfect group for people who were already overly committed. Our platform was simple and to the point: no meetings, no classes, and no fundraisers. In fact, we wouldn't do anything.

People signed up in droves. Before we were through, nearly ten thousand businesspeople had sent in for membership cards. The organization was my upbeat way of explaining personal decisions Dan and I had made concerning the roles of ambition and success in our life.

I had walked a long, eventful road during the several years that led me to that stage to stand before my biggest audience to date, a road that began the day Dan and I signed the mortgage papers on the house of our dreams. Along with many of our peers, we had bought the myth that we could have it all. On top of our sixty-hour work weeks spent running our growing public relations agency, we added one child, and then another. Propelled by our expectation that our hard work and goodness would be rewarded, we pictured the idyllic suburban setting for our growing family. There would be children romping happily on green lawns. A dog would be napping in front of the fireplace. And Dan and myself? While the ink was still wet on the mortgage papers, I had the sinking realization that we would be at the office every day of the week until nine or ten p.m. to pay off this dream. And even then, sacrificing our health and vitality to serve our increasingly demanding clients, there was no guarantee we would keep the business. Competitors come along offering bigger promises and lower prices. Clients merge, change their marketing directions, and go bankrupt. Owning our own business was a risky undertaking, but—in this chaotic age of acquisitions and downsizing—so is working for somebody else. There are no guarantees.

The youthful ambition that had fueled our race to the finish line was leaving us just when we needed it most. For as long as we could remember, we'd been using sheer willpower and effort to keep one step ahead of our financial responsibilities. We had both been honored for our contributions to the field of public relations; but Dan and I shared the feeling that our work took more from us than it gave back. The more responsibility we took on, the more that was demanded of us. We were consumed by the struggle to get new business, to help our ravenous clients meet their marketing goals, and to keep ourselves and our management team functioning sufficiently to pay for our increased overhead.

But how could we expect ourselves or our staff to try any harder, work longer, or strive for more excellence? We were already at the limit. And it was becoming obvious to us that the harder we worked, the farther behind we were falling. There was no inspiration, no joy, no creativity in this. But was this situation the result of some personal inadequacy on our part? Was there some fatal flaw built into Dan's and my psyche destined to self-destruct just at the moment of our apparent triumph?

What about those hard-edged executives we read about daily on the business pages, glibly swimming with the sharks, relentlessly searching for excellence, taking their guerilla business battles to the streets of the marketplace? Role models for ambition and success glared at us endlessly from the glossy pages of advertisements and national business magazines. People like Bill Gates, Donald Trump, Michael Miliken, and Leona Helmsley.

And then there were the movie moguls—the stars, the directors, the producers—who crowed about their latest films, their charity benefits, their fitness routines, not to mention their highly publicized deep and rich relationships with their impeccably dressed, precious children. Were we not equally worthy of the American dream?

I mentally switched channels, thinking about each of my friends and associates who likewise seemed to have it all. Our peers did precious little romping. In the case of one of our good friends, only we and his immediate family knew that even as he was being honored for being top salesperson of the year in his company, he was scrambling to replace his largest piece of business. Another friend was just about to receive a promotion when she discovered that her boss had accepted a position with another firm. Our most successful friends were showing us pictures of their recent trip to Europe when the phone rang: A competitor's new technology had just made their top product obsolete. We were all good people, working against the odds to establish a livelihood that would support ourselves and our families. But in fact, at that moment, I couldn't think of a single individual in my fast-track pack of professionals who didn't look just as beaten as I felt. We were not fulfilling our potential—we were exhausting it.

Those of us savvy enough to realize we were burning out also expected that if only we meditated, exercised, and ate enough soy, our emotions would be handled. When our attempts to be spiritual failed, we didn't just feel bad. We felt bad about feeling bad.

I took a leap. Perhaps, I surmised, the fact that trying to have it all took so much out of us was not proof of some inadequacy on our part. Rather, it could be the symptom of the unhealthy expectations and closely guarded societal illusions that had infected our times. We were doing everything by the rules—but where was meaning? Where was fulfillment? Why did I feel so alone so much of the time? Why did I so often feel so inadequate? Surely, beneath the fairytale stories of how we wish things could be, there were deeper answers that could help us make sense of things. I vowed to do whatever it would take to reclaim the time and space in my life that I knew it would require to gain the perspective I sought. There must be a better way to live and work. I would recruit Dan to help me explore and redefine ambition and success in the context of our need to make a living. We would take a step back, long enough to take a deep breath. We even had to be willing to let go of our demanding lifestyle, if that was what was necessary to buy the time for this journey. Nothing would be sacred. Not the car phone. Not the Porsche. Not even the house.

Dan wasn't thrilled. Sell the house? We'd just bought the house. But I persisted. After several more months of fervent debate, Dan finally agreed to join the revolution in earnest. We reduced the size of our business, cutting our hours back to no more than forty a week each. We were willing to pay for our newfound freedom by living in simpler circumstances. We put our dream home up for sale and made plans to move to a more modest cottage.

Extolling the virtues of simplicity, I went public with our story. Values before profit became our rallying cry, as we shared our message on *Today* and *Good Morning America*, among many others. "You can regain meaning in your work," we proclaimed. "It is worth the sacrifice to reclaim time and space in your life."

I loved to share my simple philosophy with people, telling them how we'd cut back our lifestyle to find happiness.

So why, on that balmy spring day, did I find myself facing an audience of one thousand of my peers, sweating out the living nightmare of my childhood fears?

Because just before going on stage, I had checked in with Dan, holding down the fort in San Francisco. The first quarter earnings for our company had just been phoned in by our accountant. They were up.

And this wasn't the first time.

The truth is that for nearly one full year, the trend toward downward mobility had been in reverse. Our dramatically smaller staff was handling virtually the same load of accounts we had held at the height of our master of the universe days. And we were doing this work at a comfortable pace. Our profits were exceeding industry averages month after month.

Here I was telling the finest businesspeople in one of the biggest cities in the country that there were more important things than making money, while at the same time, our bank account was reaching all-time highs. This wasn't just a matter of forgetting my steps. This, I realized mid-speech, was a matter requiring entirely new choreography. The evidence was incontestable, but hardly believable. We had sliced our hours; suggested to our staff that they cut out overtime; let go of our impressive trappings—and now we were more successful than ever. Not only that, but our zest for work had returned, and with it, the sense of purpose and meaning for which we'd yearned. We were even less afraid of the twists and turns of fate we knew lay just around every bend in the contemporary workplace. As I pondered this new information, I left a heavily weighted pause. To the sound of spoons hitting the sidewalls of ice cream dishes, I formulated the underlying principle I now call Inner Excellence that comprises the heart and soul of this book:

Personal values and quality of life considerations need not conflict with ambition and success. In fact, it is from nurturing these very qualities that your greatest experience of success will grow.

When I resumed talking, I put away my well-worn notes and began pouring out my revelations-in-process. The audience had been fully prepared to swallow the concept of reducing their lifestyles as the bitter pill of financial punishment for the spiritual rewards of incorporating personal values into their lives. But the premise of Inner Excellence I put forth in this book, as it emerged that day in the form of a stream-of-consciousness confessional, sounded like the ravings of a madwoman. *Pay attention to the nurturing of your heart and your greatest experience of success will come as a by-product of the growth of spirit.* There was polite applause at the end of the lunch. But one response on my comment cards said it all: "Get Real."

By the time I arrived home, I knew I was in for some serious reassessment. How could I continue to sell people on downward mobility while Dan and I busied ourselves putting our profits into a growing portfolio of real estate investments? How could I tell my audiences to get off the fast track while I, myself, was jetting from city to city having the time of my life giving speeches? While it was true that I had learned to find meaning in the little things — sniffing the flowers that grew in the garden, hanging my child's crayon self-portrait on our refrigerator — somewhere along the line I had rekindled my desire to make a difference in the world. And furthermore, that contribution was being recognized financially, emotionally, and spiritually.

There was no discrepancy. I knew this in my gut. But who would believe me? Even I could not yet explain why things were turning out this way. I needed to take a break from the public spotlight to give my fledgling theory about Inner Excellence time to mature. And I had to test the theory not only in the good times at hand, but against whatever the future might bring. Could it really be true that the secret to lasting success was as simple as obeying the dictates of one's own heart, trusting that everything else is details that, in their own time and way, will work themselves out?

On long walks, in meditation, and in my journal, I asked myself the tough questions. Was this some kind of fluke? Would this work for other people? Would it work for employees of corporations? Professionals in service firms? Teachers, restaurant workers, and car mechanics? Dan and I continued to run the business, testing the Principles of Inner Excellence through year after year of balance sheets. We practiced the principles shared in this book, seeing that they worked through crisis as well as triumph. Meanwhile, I attempted to put the concepts that were working so well for us into words, giving voice to what was turning out to be no less than a new work ethic for the contemporary workplace.

Over time, using our own careers and business as guinea pigs, we formulated our philosophy into seven radical principles. Unlike other success advice on the business bookshelf, the principles I share in this book are not simply techniques and strategies. These do not teach how to manipulate others for the purpose of obtaining power. Rather, they are an entry into the deeper philosophical and spiritual perspectives that shape our relationship to ambition, success, and meaning.

They provide the foundation of understanding that must be acknowledged before any of the more superficial management strategies and advice available in the marketplace can function for other than temporary gain.

As thousands of individuals have applied these principles to their own lives, we have had the opportunity to see how they work in many companies and workplace situations in addition to our own. From accountants to middle managers, from artists to contractors, from dentists to retailers: The Principles of Inner Excellence apply.

The conclusion many of us have been astonished by is what I will share with you in this book. *The more you pay attention to the caretaking of your spirit, the greater the experience of success you will have.* You can find what you've been searching for, regardless of the circumstances with which you are faced. In many cases, you will work less and achieve more. In all cases, you will find meaning and purpose, no matter what. You may find a thousand reasons why, while these precepts may have worked for us, they won't work for you. They can work for you anyway. Prepare to be surprised.

Chapter Two

Life-Driven Work

In order to find a lasting experience of success in unstable times, you must learn to tap into new, life-driven sources of inspiration, creativity, and vitality.

raditional approaches to "making it" no longer work in the contemporary workplace. Before exploring the reasons for this, let us consider what these traditional approaches entail.

The owner of a chain of restaurants invited me to hear his keynote address at their annual management meeting. The story he shared—a motivational classic— puts us in the general philosophical barnyard:

> Once upon a time, a chicken and a pig bumped into each other.
> "I'm more important than you are," bragged the pig.
> "Oh no you're not," replied the chicken. "Whenever the master wants breakfast, he always calls on me."
> The pig sneered.
> "That's just the point. When it comes to breakfast, the difference between you and me is that you partici- pate—but I'm commited."

After all the employees laughed for a sufficient length of time, the owner of the chain concluded his story by adding that we should all be like the pig, fully committed.

After the session, he asked me what I thought of his presentation.

"The point of the story is that you want us to be committed—like the pig?" I mustered up my courage as best I could. After all, this was a client who represented a fair amount of revenue to our firm. "But Stan," I said, lowering my voice to a whisper, "the pig dies."

Stan is a reasonable man. He is a good father to his children—when he sees them for a couple of hours every other weekend or so. He respects his wife—when he can catch glimpses of her between her charity fundraisers, dedicated to assisting the restaurant chain in keeping its high community profile. He even cares about his employees—when they bring in the numbers he sets for them.

But Stan is caught up in a web of business practices and philosophies, spoken and unspoken, that cause him to hold up self-destructive ideals for himself and his employees on a daily basis.

When Stan grew up, in the decades when the Horatio Alger myth still had some real juice in it, the presumption was that hard work would be rewarded with success. It is a simple formula, holding great sway with those of us who grew up in its shadow. If only it had proven to be true.

Facing increased competition from too many people fighting for too few slots—first in the finer colleges, then for jobs, now for promotions in the truncated corporate pyramids that have stalled more than one fine career—we have made the forty-hour work week, for which most of us are paid, an anachronism. Fifty- and sixty-hour work weeks (which in the day of the gray flannel suit were a sign of the divinely inspired—or at least the divinely driven) have become the norm. Now, to work harder and longer, one must differentiate one's self from the competition by working around the clock. Our clients in the hotel business have always understood this concept. For them, the client literally moves in. There are no vacations and no weekends. In fact, one of the primary perks offered top hotel management is housing on the premises.

For the rest of us, living in the age of the global economy, stock markets around the world determining the value of the change in our pockets even while we sleep, the twenty-four hour day has become a literal reality.

A trip to the newsstand can reveal a frightening portrait of contemporary success. In glossy advertisements in our major business and news magazines, executives can find their favorite clothing store still open at 10 p.m., ready to press their clothes for their next round of meetings. Then it's off to the airport, arriving at the hotel at 2 a.m. to be greeted by an urgent fax. The deal is concluded by long-distance phone, overseas, at 3 a.m. We are on the fast track to success, briefcases flying, heels on fire, gasping for air. These images are not the personification of inspiration. Scratch the surface of the quest for excellence, and you will find anxiety and fear. Over the past decade, the driven pace of the American workplace has surpassed the limits of human endurance. The old strategies for success—trying harder and working smarter, providing service or product above what the competition is also trying to deliver—have, quite simply, broken down.

In the case of Stan's chain of restaurants, the implications of his inspirational story were immediate and terrible. After listening to the story of the chicken and the pig, the managers of the restaurants in the chain left the smoke-filled room to fight the good fight. Whenever I stopped by any of their sites, morning, night, weekends, I saw them giving their all. On deeper inspection, I learned that a number of them were fueling their all with uppers and cocaine.

By the time the next marketing meeting rolled around, one of the managers had proven to be just as committed as the pig. While on the job, he suffered a fatal heart attack, leaving behind a wife and several young children.

Recently, I was invited to be a keynote speaker before an association of hospital-based nurses. After my talk, one of the nurses came up to me with tears in her eyes.

"I've never admitted this to anybody," she began. "But I am so exhausted, so much of the time, I'm actually jealous of the patients. All I want to do is lie down and rest, and if my body were to breakdown, I'd finally have an excuse to stop. I know that this is sick thinking, but this is just my point. Many of the patients are healthier than the staff that is serving them."

Living up to our society's role models for success, we give everything we've got — and more. Isn't it ironic, then, that despite our extraordinary commitment to our careers and businesses, so many of our major industries and institutions are in shambles? What have we accomplished with all this commitment? We have done little more than create a workforce that is unhealthy and dispirited. Deprived by our anxiety-driven pace of the subtler human qualities that would otherwise provide perspective and meaning, we find ourselves in a fear-driven, reactive mode. Companies with healthy-enough bottom lines lay off one-third of their workforce in fear-driven anticipation of what the future might bring, leaving both those who are terminated and those who remain in desperate situations. Manufacturers send executives to far-flung outposts around the world, looking for cheaper suppliers, turning U.S. workplaces into ghost towns. Uncomfortable mergers, the norm rather than the exception, pit corporate cultures against one another. Motivated by fear, we grab what we can for ourselves, establishing the destructive reciprocities that eventually result in a society dominated by greed and self-interest. And experts tell us that the pressure from outside ourselves to keep up the pace will only increase over the coming years.

At the restaurant manager's funeral, everybody blamed increasing competition in the marketplace for the pressure he and they were under—too many new restaurants, escalating food prices, not enough good help. And yet, the greatest stress on that organization had less to do with these external factors and more to do with massive turnover caused by burnout, dismissal for drug use, and now death. It had to do with poor interpersonal relationships between managers and staff, fueled by resentment and guilt. And it had to do with the impact of fear and stress on the manager's ability to think clearly and creatively.

In a survey of those on my mailing list, I asked the question, "Do you think at some point, working harder and longer can become counterproductive?"

I had several hundred responses, coming from twenty industries in twelve states. My correspondents included people who worked in manufacturing, utility companies, aerospace, and high-tech companies; technical professionals, such as mechanical engineers and lab technicians; healthcare workers, including doctors, psychologists, and nurses. There were real estate salespeople, photographers, secretaries, and presidents.

The response was unanimous:

"Working harder and longer can lead to desperation, which leads to panic and then loss of confidence and self-control. Who could succeed feeling those feelings?"

"A slower, more realistic way of scheduling work is more productive in the long run. There are fewer mistakes, fewer false starts, better concentration, higher morale, and greater creativity. This shows up directly in the quality of results."

"We have got to have uninterrupted time to think and create. You can't get this if you are working for somebody who is willing to sacrifice their own sanity, not to mention yours, for the sake of short-term gains. It is the job of people in management to model a healthy life with time for work, relationships, recreation, creativity, and so on. Then work can take on an appropriate role in our lives."

Just as we give hurricanes names, the Japanese have given death from overwork a name. They call it *karoshi*. But hurricanes and *karoshi* have a big difference. Globalization and increased competition, however awesome they seem to those of us perched on the brink, are not natural phenomena. We forget that every reason offered to justify the pressure on us to explore the outer reaches of human endurance derives from phenomena that are strictly, unequivocably man-made. We can't stop hurricanes from happening. But we can do something about *karoshi*.

If you had participated in my survey, I feel certain that you would have answered similarly to those who responded. Of course you know that the pace at which you are working is counterproductive. You know what it takes for you to be truly productive. So why don't you make the necessary changes?

Because to do so, you must adopt new ways of thinking that run counter to virtually every precept of traditional western business philosophy. Taking the leap necessary to implement the principles in this book may be, in fact, a desperate act. In this regard, then—providing the impetus for taking the risk—desperation may actually serve a useful purpose.

It was out of desperation, for instance, that Dan and I gave up turning to traditional business management and inspiration books for advice. These best-selling books were full of advice teaching us how to swim with the sharks, search for excellence, and be an s.o.b. But what good was it to have our top business experts tell us that the way to gain the edge was to work harder and longer than our competitors if our competitors were reading the same books? We ransacked the shelves of our local bookstores, bypassing the business books and finding our way to alternative sources of inspiration.

Amazingly, it was saints, heroes, and mystics from times long past whose insights and parables offered the most concrete and immediately applicable advice to guide our transition. From myth to literature, from folklore to history: We began the task of translating esoteric images into the language of contemporary business success.

Although we brandished the briefcase of the executive rather than the sword of the hero, I came to realize that we were just as surely on a heroic quest. The prize we seek may be to find a better way to make a living, rather than the Golden Fleece, but I soon began to understand that the hero's internal process was the same for us in today's workplace as it was for heroes of ages long past. The challenges we face in our careers and businesses are now, as it was for the heroes back then, essentially spiritual in nature.

The word spirituality connotes many things to many people, so I will define it carefully. In this book, spirituality refers to that deeply alive place within each of us that longs for fulfillment. This inner longing, when acknowledged, can be a task master far more demanding than the external prods to action that many of us currently allow to call the shots in our busy lives. Envisioned as a wall of fire or a fierce dragon, heroic spirituality calls us forth to meet life on life's terms.

You must find qualities within yourself you did not know you possessed.

You must be willing to surrender your past understandings about what it means to be a powerful person to discover the source of real strength.

You must be willing to venture beyond your own comfort zone to journey where no one has ever gone before: into the inner recesses of your own heart.

I am not talking about leaving the world of ambition and success to find peace by escaping to a less demanding life. I am talking about being willing to venture inward to find new sources of inspiration for practical application in your life. When it is inspiration rather than fear that is the primary motivation for your livelihood, you will be applying the Seven Principles of Inner Excellence to your everyday life.

Courage to make the shift from a fear-driven to inspiration-driven motivation is required because of our society's bias against looking within for alternatives. Spirituality, the cynics will tell you, is that touchy-feely stuff that may belong in a place of worship, but certainly has no place in serious work environments. Spirituality is for the soft-hearted, they say, who retreat into their hearts because they don't have the stuff it takes to make it in the real world.

Psychologist Abraham Maslow explained that this prejudice against looking within is a function of the psychosocial orientation of western culture. From religion to politics, from science to academia, we have been taught not to trust ourselves — not to trust that we do know what we most deeply desire and that we know how to resolve our inner conflicts. We have been taught that beneath the veneer of the socialized conscious mind lurks who-knows-what animal urges, repressed hostilities, and other evils.

The irony is that we are all spiritual beings. We all have ideas about how the world works and our place in it. We have yearnings for understanding and meaning in our lives and work. Whether your ideas about how the world works are endorsed by the church or the marketplace, whether you hold them consciously or unconsciously, the beliefs you possess will have a big impact on the way you talk about your career, the decisions you make, and your responses to the things that happen to you. Every feeling, every interaction is determined by what kind of universe you think this is. Is the world a friendly place, guided by a loving, divine presence? Or are you strictly on your own, left to duke it out on lawless streets?

The question, which will be explored more fully in the discussion of Principle Number One, is not whether or not you are a spiritual person, but whether the spiritual beliefs you hold are working for or against the things you really want to have in your life.

People who want to avoid taking the leap within can find many means at their disposal to do so. The yearning for meaning can be temporarily abated by drinking, taking drugs, overeating, and overworking. When things get uncomfortable in one job, rather than explore how you might be contributing to the difficulties, jump to another where—at least for a day or two—you'll be comforted by the illusion that you've left your troubles behind you. Or, on the other hand, you could simply stay in a repressive situation far longer than you should, rationalizing a thousand reasons why you have to stay. Often, it seems easier to ignore the voice of wisdom than to pay heed to what your heart is asking of you.

Over the past several years, I have become friends with a number of my fellow doctoral students in the department of religion. The traditional definition of success in this context is to progress as rapidly as possible through coursework, exams, and dissertation to win the coveted Ph.D. and ultimately a prestigious professorship. Joseph was one doctoral candidate who had been dying to quit the program for several years. By the time he realized that he disliked just about everything concerning academics—from interdepartmental politics to the pressure to achieve to the emphasis on intellect over spirit—he had already invested a significant amount of time and money into the program. It was obvious to all who knew Joseph that even if he were to succeed at pushing himself to completion, he would literally make a miserable professor. But even under the gentlest of suggestions along these lines, he would bristle. Clearly, he didn't want to talk about it. But why? One day, opening a rare crack into his inner processes, Joseph made a confession.

"I've got too much invested in this. If I quit now, my ego couldn't take it. My best bet is to get through this as quickly as possible and not think about it too much."

Cynthia, another friend in the program, took a different route. While Cynthia sometimes looked at those like Joseph who were progressing towards the doctorate on schedule with envy, she did not have the facility to push herself through the hard places without pause. For Cynthia, the hard places made inner demands upon her that were equal to the intellectual work of the doctorate itself. Was she truly called to teach? How would she handle the politics that she knew would only increase as her career progressed? Would it be better for her to find meaning in less painful ways? Sometimes her answers were clear and immediate. Sometimes Cynthia needed to ponder and mull before getting back on track. In fact, so as not to push herself according to external pressures rather than to the slower pace of her own internal enfolding, she went to work part-time doing flower arrangements for a local florist, taking fewer courses than expected. While before long Joseph was being applauded for the timely completion of his doctorate and his appointment to a prestigious professorship, some of my classmates were quick to judge Cynthia a failure. But I did not agree.

Unless he changed his relationship to work, Joseph was most probably going to pay for the appearance of rapid success with a lifetime of making do with a professorship that looked good from the outside, but that he hated. When and where would he finally take stock of his life? Stop taking orders from his ego and start listening to his heart?

On the other hand, I trusted that if and when Cynthia completed her doctorate, she would have already asked and answered all the tough questions. She would be prepared mentally, spiritually, and emotionally for the demands of her chosen profession. She would be sure it was something she wanted to do and that the sacrifices and drawbacks would still be worth it. At the same time, she could yet decide to throw in the towel on the doctorate and concentrate on flower arranging for her livelihood. Whatever she chose would be the right decision for her and would bring her great happiness.

Who is really the success? Who is the failure?

Three thousand years ago, the *I Ching*, the Chinese book of philosophy, explained to its students that once individuals face the fear of looking honestly into their own hearts, they will never fear any threat that comes from outside themselves again.

This advice holds the key to power, with direct practical application to your career, business, and life; but the door it unlocks is to a humility that seems the very antithesis of our contemporary understanding of ambition and success. What do I mean by humility? I mean that we give up worrying about what others think of us. We allow ourselves to look foolish and feel vulnerable. We heed the dictates of our hearts and accept the consequences. Joseph looked to all the world like he was doing just this: delaying gratification to achieve a greater goal. But the truth is that he was denying his own heart and stifling his spirit. However great his accomplishments, they will only be a shadow of his true potential—if only he had chosen to motivate his ambition through inspiration and love rather than through ego and fear.

Is it worth the risk to open this door? If you truly want to have the experience and not just the appearance of success, what is your alternative? You are already bright enough, educated enough; you have already worked hard enough and long enough; you have already striven for excellence enough. You have done enough of what is no longer working for you. Do you want to find meaning and fulfillment in your worklife? Then you're going to have to try something new.

Chapter Three

Reclaiming Our Human Resources

The unrest you are experiencing is not individual psychological difficulty, but rather part of a wider spiritual awakening.

After the restaurant manager's funeral, Stan called his staff and consultants together to give us a pep talk.

"With Kevin gone, we are going to have to pull together and work even harder to reach our goals."

Not long thereafter, the chain received a second blow. One of the country's prominent restaurant review guidebooks downgraded the restaurant's rating, taking away one of their coveted stars. Despite the fact that the downgrading was clearly due to the restaurant's rocky culinary performance, Stan instead chose to blame the public relations agency executive we had assigned to the account. Good publicity can do a lot. But it can't make up for a kitchen in chaos, run by frightened people salving their nerves with alcohol and cocaine. After a profitable ten-year relationship, and a number of attempts to wake our client up, I resigned representation of Stan's restaurant chain. Still Stan did not get the message. Those who persist in driving their careers and businesses at break-neck speeds are sooner or later going to have an accident. The Big Eight accounting firms, the airlines, the savings and loan industry, healthcare: The beginning of the millennium looks more like an army surplus warehouse for obsolete and wrecked vehicles than the noble economic battlefield in which we had been geared for combat.

The fact that you are reading these principles today is not a coincidence. The negative effects of dysfunctional beliefs about success have snowballed over the past decade. More and more of us are bridling beneath the anxiety-fueled motivations that may provide the appearance of success in the short-term. But over time, these motivations have proven to take more from us than they contribute. A few years ago, I ran a contest to find the country's most overworked executive. There were hundreds of entries from around the country, most of whom clocked in at eighty- or ninety-hour work weeks or more. The winner was Jack, a middle manager from a multinational corporation's Manhattan office. He hadn't submitted his own name. That was his wife's doing. She was concerned that if something did not grab Jack's attention soon, he would go the way of the pig. You see, he had already had a series of heart attacks. He was so committed to work that he kept a packed overnight bag next to his desk should he start to feel chest pains. His portable computer, complete with modem, scanner, and printer, would allow him to continue to operate his affairs out of a hospital bed. He not only did this once, but a series of times — until his wife's letter reached contest headquarters.

Jack was simultaneously bemused and chagrined. He graciously agreed to participate in a New York City press conference at which he would formally accept the prize: a year's supply of roses, delivered one month at a time. (He needed to supply the time to smell them, however.) But no, he wasn't going to make any major changes in his life or work.

The day before the press event, I got a phone call. Jack was back in the hospital, his heart acting up under the increased pressure of national scrutiny. Would I mind rescheduling the press conference?

I cancelled the press conference and sent Jack the first flowers. He got the point. Several months later, I heard from him. He'd decided to take early retirement and enjoy the time he had left with his wife and family. Last I heard from Jack, he was doing fine and had plans to move to the country.

What happened to Jack was remarkable—but hardly unique. The notion is occurring to an increasing number of us that the troubles we are encountering in our out-of-control worklives are not the result of individual psychological difficulty. Rather, we are beginning to see our dissatisfaction with the way things are as part of a wider awakening. Many of us who have experienced some degree of success recognize that we have had unprecedented mobility, access to expanded resources and information—and the education to appreciate and use them. Many of us are using information drawn from other times and places as a springboard for our emerging beliefs. What in many other societies would have constituted "secret knowledge," garbed in esoteric language and obtuse imagery available only to an elite, is available for all of us to incorporate into our everyday lives. The thousands of individuals who are responding to the call for a new work ethic are harbingers of a new era for business, an age when personal values, spirit, and integrity are not checked at the door as we hit our workplaces. We are demonstrating every day that the approach embodied in the Seven Principles of Inner Excellence has practical, profitable implications.

With this spirit to spark the fuse, the American business mainstream is destined to experience no less than a revolution in the way we approach our careers and companies. Practicing the Principles of Inner Excellence, people work at a pace that enhances their vitality, allowing them the time to refuel themselves with self-nurturing. Employers and employees keep the lines of communication open and honest, understanding that overall, the needs of the individual are consistent with what is best for the business. This cannot be accomplished in an environment motivated primarily by fear. Anxiety and stress over time decrease our ability to perform. Only in an environment inspired by the practice of inner excellence can we hope to fulfill our potential, and not only as workers—but as human beings.

We need not only new beliefs, but new behaviors. And while it is always welcome when healthy change starts at the top, this movement has made major in-roads at every level of the American workplace.

In my mailed survey, I also asked the question, "Can you think of ways your company/affiliation has been able to reduce anxiety in the workplace?"

"In our office," one of my correspondents wrote, "when someone reports that they are home with the flu, I am pretty certain that I won't stumble across them at the baseball game, or out shopping with their children."

Why? Because this person works for one of a growing number of companies who have instituted mental health days in addition to vacation or sick time where individuals in any position can choose to spend time away from the office to revitalize without guilt or subterfuge.

Employees at one firm asked if the study of aikido could be offered as part of the firm's professional development program. At another firm, employees got permission to turn an empty office into a meditation room.

Many correspondents reported replacing the power lunch, with its time-consuming quasi-social ambiance, with a quiet solo stroll through the corporate environs, utilizing the precious midday moments to relax and revitalize rather than perform or entertain. Workers committed to inner excellence trust that they will have the time and energy to build a fulfilling life outside of normal work hours. As a result, the time spent in meetings about meetings and complaining about each other at the water cooler can instead be invested in activities during the workday more to the point of accomplishing goals.

To handle the unavoidable pressures of a county assessor's office, one creative group of civil servants initiated a quiet-time policy for the eighty-person office. Six of the workers screen phone calls and handle customers from 8:30 a.m. to 10:30 a.m. every day. Doors are closed and meetings are postponed. Everyone, with the exception of the rotating six on call, has uninterrupted time. By five months after initiation of the program, staff reported that the backlog of work had been considerably reduced.

At our company, people are encouraged to leave the office at a decent hour and to use their full vacation time. When they are sitting at their desks looking overwhelmed by stacks of work, they are not prodded to work faster, harder, or longer. We act on the theory that if the company is staffed adequately, employees will find the solution to handling the backup within the normal workday more readily through support and trust than through fear and desperation. To staff adequately, however, requires that we not only react to but anticipate shifting workloads and that we resist the temptation to become greedy. This is the key to running a less-stressed company in today's economy: to operate sensitively on the fulcrum between too little and too much. The *I Ching* describes the ideal balance as a pot of water set to boil over a fire. If the fire's too low, the water won't boil. If it's too high, the water evaporates. Only when the relationship between the fire and the pot is just right can the water be free to do its most effective work.

The ideal is for each of us to be free to choose the appropriate and most productive level of energy to invest in our work at any given time. Each member of the team has the willingness and capacity to rise to the occasion, whatever that occasion might be. People who are fortunate enough to find a culture that understands the Principles of Inner Excellence report that working in such an environment actually inspires them to exceed previous levels of commitment. Our company is one among a growing number of workplaces that honors outside hobbies and interests, bending as we can to accommodate requests for flex-time, job-sharing, and other creative options.

There are, of course, periods when producing at the outer reaches of endurance and ability for an extended period of time is necessary and even nurturing. I do not, for instance, regret the long hours I invested in the early years of building our business or rising to the occasion today when our clients have special needs. I have no problem burning the midnight oil when driven by inspiration to do the demanding research for a new book or to take advantage of a marketing opportunity.

At the same time, working in highly competitive industries, it would be dishonest to give the impression that we are never driven by the pressure of impossible deadlines and unreasonable clients' demands. At these times if it isn't fear that brings home paperwork to tackle after my daughter Jody gets her goodnight kiss, it is something that does a pretty good imitation of it.

The real problem comes, however, when I—or any of us—go into unconscious overdrive, forgetting to shift back out of high gear after such a bout with adrenaline has served its purpose.

Steve, a media buyer in a southern city close to ours, gave us his résumé just a few months after landing what he thought was the job of his dreams in one of the region's top advertising agencies. He loved the work, he reported, but his boss, the CEO, was one such adrenaline junkie. For this hyped-up man, every day was a crisis. Steve was often asked to work nights and weekends. Exhausted, he stole some time away from the office for a guilty cup of coffee.

"It's not that I am unwilling to work hard and long," he explained. "But if I do, I want it to be for some real purpose."

To illustrate his complaint, he shared with us the story of what happened at their company during one of the south's rare, debilitating icestorms. Because the city is unequipped for serious winter weather, all but the main roads became impassable. Cars lay like beached whales at the bottom of hills, unable to make the climb. Organizations rescheduled their meetings and all the public schools were cancelled.

On this particularly bleak day, electricity was out all over the city. The air was filled with the sound of cracking branches and tree limbs, buckling dangerously under the weight of the ice. Steve and his family huddled around the fire listening to the battery-operated radio. Then the phone rang.

"Where are you?" his boss asked.

"You mean, you're at the office and you want me to come in?" Steve asked in astonishment.

"Officially, the company's closed. But those of us who are serious about serving our clients somehow made it in. Don't you have a four-wheel drive vehicle?"

"Yes."

"Then come on down."

Steve explained to us that it took him two hours, dodging downed power lines, immobile cars, and emergency road vehicles, to make the run that under normal circumstances takes about fifteen minutes. Even that would have been alright with him. But when he got to the office, the handful of people who'd made it in were huddled around a candle in a dark conference room, waiting for the electricity to be restored. The moment he saw the office, computers dead in the dark, he realized that this had been a test of loyalty and grit—having nothing to do with serving the clients' needs, emergency or otherwise. Recognizing that this was his boss's pattern, and not an exception, he made the decision to seek an environment that was not only committed to the appearance of success—but to the health and well-being of its employees.

Most of us are willing to respond to genuine emergencies or opportunities. The real problem comes when, like Steve's boss, we rise to the occasion and then forget to come back down again. Entire industries—healthcare and journalism, to name two—have gone into permanent high-gear to the detriment of everybody involved.

From the outside, the inspiration-driven workplace or career may look no different from one that is fueled by fear or greed. People are at their desks, busy at work. Phones are ringing. Packages are delivered, deadlines are kept.

Recently, I received a phone call from a job applicant, scheduled to have arrived for her interview with me twenty minutes earlier.

"I'm behind on my schedule today," she reported cheerily. "I started to panic, until I realized who it was I was going to be meeting. I was certain you would understand if I chose not to make myself crazy rushing around and came to see you an hour late."

"I understand," I replied. "But I won't be here."

The Principles of Inner Excellence are not about lowering standards or results. They are about the reclamation of vitality, creativity, and natural inspiration from that most important of business assets: our human resources.

Take the case of a factory owner in Massachusetts. Crunching some numbers, he realized that the company's sales had picked up significantly. At the same time, his workers had responded to the pressure to produce by pushing their hours to the point that ten-hour days had become the norm. Taking a closer look, he realized that no more was being produced in the ten-hour days than had been produced in the bygone era of eight-hour days before business picked up. Not only that, there were more accidents and morale was down. The owner ended overtime for factory and office workers and scheduled a second shift. It cost him more in salaries, but he believed that by revitalizing his workforce, he would in the end get a more efficient factory floor. *Inc.* magazine reported that accidents declined. Soon he was able to issue his workers three extra paychecks a year, made possible by higher productivity.

In such an environment, bosses and employees are much more apt to be creative, to take reasonable risks, and to derive personal satisfaction from work.

Companies who believe in these principles are still relatively few in number, but the number is growing rapidly. As CEOs come to realize that there can be a positive correlation between these principles and the bottom line, we will see the inner excellence business philosophy become the number one perk of the coming decades.

Just as in the past, when high-tech and financial companies competed for employees by appealing to greed, companies are now discovering that the way to win the top candidates is with promises of flexible schedules, on-site childcare, and extracurricular activities, like company choirs and reading clubs. But to be truly effective, inner excellence is not just about adding things on top of a dysfunctional culture. It is about changing the culture itself.

David, a management consultant, was asked to give a talk before a dispirited group of supervisors in a defense industry manufacturing company on the subject of "Motivating From the Inside Out." The talk was scheduled for 3:30 p.m. David knew that the company had been going through radical downsizing—their work force had been cut from 4,000 to 1,700 over the past several years. He began his talk by asking a key question.

"Do you want to inspire your workers? First ask yourself, are you inspired yourself?"

David spoke about the fact that in crisis, many companies slap motivation programs like Band-Aids over cultures that are riddled with distrust.

"Companies working on morale issues demand that their workers go play pool together after work in order to bond, when the employees would much rather be at home with their families."

When he finished the first part of his talk, the room was dead silent. He asked for questions. There were none. What had gone wrong? When it came time for the break, he decided to pass out the feedback forms he normally saved for the end of the day. This way, he could make adjustments based on what the group was feeling.

When he gathered the forms up, he was astonished. The comments were overwhelmingly positive. So why had the group been so silent?

One comment, scribbled in the margins, said it all.

"What you're saying is so true and so painful, I was speechless. Did you know that our workday goes from 7:00 a.m. to 3:30 p.m.? We were asked to stay late for this."

The human resources people who had neglected to mention this were chagrined by David's feedback. Subsequent to his talk, they took a step in the right direction. The least they could do, they realized, was to initiate workshops and bonding experiences within the workday—going so far as to hire temps and reduce workloads on those days so that the workers at the manufacturing facility would no longer be inadvertantly punished when the true intention was to nurture and motivate.

In his book *Love and Profit: The Art of Caring Leadership*, businessman James A. Autry explains that in order to make our work communities function in a healthy, vital way, we must go beyond manipulation and come to truly care for one another. Autry, who headed the Meredith Corporation for many years, envisions the workplace as a neighborhood in which most of us spend a good part of our lives.

"My businessman friend knows that his business is better when his relationships are better," Autry writes about one of his mentors. As opposed to those managers who use fear-based techniques and strategies to direct people to perform for the company's interest, Autry writes for "those who approach management as a calling, a life engagement that, if done properly, combines technical and administrative skills with vision, compassion, honesty, and trust to create an environment in which people can grow personally, can feel fulfilled, can contribute to the common good, and can share in the psychic and financial rewards of a job well done."

Autry's ideal manager does not just sit at his or her desk "waiting for someone to screw up so they'll have something to do." Autry's manager is engaged, vulnerable, and trusting. Understanding the risk involved, Autry begins every exchange with the presumption of goodwill. While such a presumption makes him vulnerable to those individuals who would abuse his respect and trust, Autry explains that the alternative is to shut yourself off from your compassion and humanity. That is a cost that is quite simply unacceptable to him. Autry writes: "In every office you hear the threads of love and joy and fear and guilt, the cries for celebration and reassurance, and somehow you know that connecting those threads is what you are supposed to do and business takes care of itself."

Autry is someone who truly understands the meaning of inner excellence: the realization that personal values, integrity, caring about others, and quality of life considerations need not conflict with ambition and success. But we can't all work for James Autry and maybe not even any of the thousands of individuals and companies who have taken up the Seven Principles of Inner Excellence over the years.

What about the rest of us? Few of us own our own companies. And most of us can't simply shift jobs because we don't like our boss. We may know what we'd like to do, but not have the resources to make our dreams a reality. We may work in an individual corporate culture or even an entire industry that is permeated by fear.

There is an answer. The Seven Principles of Inner Excellence that comprise the heart of this book will point the way.

Part Two

❧

The Seven Principles of Inner Excellence

Principle Number One

Change your beliefs about the nature of business and of life, and you will change how you manage your worklife.

———

While we are waiting for our contemporary worklife to catch up with our philosophical ideals, the vast majority of us have bosses who are too demanding, clients who are too unappreciative. We need the income. Our families depend on us. We have responsibilities.

And underneath all of this, we also have our deeply held beliefs.

The beliefs you hold about the nature of business and of life determine how you will manage your career. Scholar and philosopher Joseph Campbell, in an important conversation with Bill Moyers (*The Power of Myth*), described our beliefs as the software of our life's computer. You enter the data, and the computer responds according to your commands. Campbell admitted that he "likes to play with the software," adding new ideas as they cross his path. Moyers suggested that some of the greatest saints borrowed from anywhere they could.

"They have taken from this and from that, and constructed a new software."

If after reading through this principle, you realize that the software you've installed is inadequate—or even destructive—you, too, can add new ideas as they cross your path. Change your beliefs and you will change how you live your life.

To reprogram your belief system, you must be prepared to hang in for the long run. You must be willing to discard what hasn't been working, look for better alternatives, take the risk of installing them, and work out the bugs. You won't just do this once. You will have to work at it over time.

The fact that installing a new set of beliefs takes time and effort runs counter to the slick and easy faith we encounter in our media-fueled world of junk food theology: just enough wisdom to sate our appetite, but not enough to offer long-term nourishment. We like our spirituality packaged for us by celebrity experts with just enough snappy stories to make them good talk show guests. Gurus offer spontaneous enlightenment at the tap of a peacock feather. We are set up for dramatic, instantaneous transformation—unprepared for the reality of the commitment it takes to program new software into our lives.

The irony is that in spiritual belief systems, you are asked to exert the greatest investment of energy, discipline, and commitment when you have the least evidence that it will be worth it. As anyone who has struggled with the reluctance to adopt new technology knows, as long as the desire for comfort and familiarity takes precedence over the potential benefits, you will resist the upgrade.

In spiritual belief systems, as in software, you progress only when you are willing to take a leap of faith that it will, in the long run, be worth it to you. Bringing your internal programming to awareness is not an easy task. It is the very pervasiveness of your assumptions that blind you to them. If you hold your worldview unconsciously, you will be the victim of your beliefs. You will have no choice about critical factors that determine your actions and responses on a day-to-day basis. The alternative is to bring them to consciousness through honesty and self-evaluation. Only then will you have a say about the assumptions that you ultimately choose to adopt that will color your decisions and behavior on the job and in your life.

The philosopher William James once wrote that taking a leap of faith is similar to the experience of a novice climbing the Alps for the first time. It is as if you find yourself in a situation in which the only escape is a terrifying leap across an abyss. Having had no experience with such a leap in the past, you have no basis upon which to assess your ability to survive the effort. But, he notes, that hope will put you in a better frame of mind to succeed than if you were riddled with fear. James writes: "Believe, and you shall be right, for you shall save yourself; doubt, and you shall be right, for you shall perish. The only difference is that to believe is greatly to your advantage."

What do you have to lose? You have already done enough of what hasn't worked for you. You've worked hard and become smart, tough, lean, and mean: And still you wonder what life is all about. How about shifting to a new way of thinking that at least holds the possibility of delivering to you that for which you yearn? As James writes, "To believe is greatly to your advantage."

What kinds of beliefs would best be left behind—and what new ones should we seek to program in?

Dan and I were once invited to a blues bash, given by a prominent lawyer for his clients and friends. Chatting our way around the room, we were able to catch snippets of conversation.

A seasoned executive shared his wisdom with a young associate, who leaned eagerly toward his mentor at the bar.

"If you are going to succeed, you've got to put the demands of your job first."

"Susan is serious about her career," the female half of a couple commented between sips. "She's always working."

Above the cool jazz tones, two men in pinstripes bragged about the fierce marketing battle their firm had waged against a competitor.

"Business is like war," one exclaimed.

"It's us or it's them," the second agreed.

Taking some well-earned R & R in this cozy environment of blues and booze, many of these businesspeople — had they been challenged — would have defined themselves as "realists." As realists, we adopt and act on assumptions that appear to us to be universally accepted as true.

Unfortunately, in our society — as reflected in the statements overheard at our associate's soiree — the primary impetus for our ambition is externally motivated.

"He who works hardest, longest, and toughest wins."

Is business a fearsome battlefield, and your clients, your employees, your bosses, and peers — not to mention your family and friends — the inevitable casualties? A customer makes an unwarranted harsh demand and you are thrust into overdrive, fending off the attack. You are unfairly passed over for a promotion and you seek revenge. You compete with your fellow workers to get on top. You fight for market share, "beat the competition" at all costs . . . and hold beliefs that allow you to make self-destructive decisions over and over again.

A young driver was sent to guide me through a maze of media interviews in Seattle. On a tight schedule, she panicked at the first stoplight over whether she could get us to our next appointment on time. Our car careened into the front drive of a television station parking lot, with a few precious moments to spare.

"Follow me!" she shouted, jumping out and disappearing around the corner of the production facility. We were in a dead run.

"Around here!" she rounded corner number two. "It's just a little farther."

As she disappeared once again, I heard her voice dimly in the distance: "It's the next one" wafted back to me from around corner three.

We were back exactly where we had begun: at the front entrance where the door to the studio had been all along.

We both survived this tangle with desperation. But not everyone is this lucky. A New York art director was given the on-going responsibility for delivering boards to one of the most demanding clients in the business. Getting them there on time could mean keeping his job.

On this particular day, he was hailing a cab when he suffered a stroke. As he fell, he maneuvered himself in such a way that he landed on the wet, dirty snow, managing to keep his client's paste-up boards dry.

A hand-scrawled poster on one of my client's bulletin boards reads:

"We don't need any more desperation, thank you. We are already oversupplied."

If it is true that you are getting sick and tired of being chased through your worklife with fear biting at your heels, why are you so willing to accept anxiety-induced motivation as the primary fuel for your ambition? Why do you contribute to a workplace environment that is unhealthy for us all?

This is not just a rhetorical question. There are reasons. We can begin to get a handle on what these reasons are by observing how many of our work culture's popular beliefs come disguised in seductive packaging, not unlike the Sirens luring Odysseus's crew to death with their irresistible voices. In the contemporary success mythology, the Sirens call out to us again—and the songs they sing are, "Work hard and you will be rewarded," and "You deserve to have it all."

From the time you are old enough to understand that the jolly old man with the fat tummy only brings presents to good little girls and boys, you get the picture about reward and punishment. You are processed through grammar school grading systems, textbook fables, and childhood heroes, not to mention well-meaning parents exacting disciplined behavior from you in exchange for love. Heaven awaits those of us who get the message—be good and things will turn out for you.

You grow up believing that if you could only be good enough, work hard enough, get it right enough you could turn your ambitions into reality. Tell enough people that if they try hard enough they can control their destinies, and what do you get? A society of superachievers, running as fast as we can but getting nowhere because we are struggling so hard to hold back the possibility that anything not to our custom-ordered expectations will happen to us. By setting ourselves in competition with one another, all we've managed to do is raise the bar concerning what it takes to succeed.

The real irony is that the closer you are to achieving your goals, the more fervently you engage in this struggle. You have done so much, you are so close to "having it all," that you actually believe that giving that extra ounce of energy and effort might close the gap. In fact, this was the bait that led me into the mega work week: not being hopelessly far behind, but rather, being so tantalizingly close. We run our lives on the "if/then" continuum. "If" I get the promotion, gain acceptance for my child into the right school, land the right mate, "then" I will be a success. But the goal, even when achieved, does not fully satisfy—for reality, even that externally-defined reality called "success," is never perfect. Your promotion requires that you spend more time traveling than is good for your personal relationships. Your child hates her teacher. There is always some flaw. Every "then" spawns a new "if" and the chase for perfect success is on again.

The impulse to perform is advanced by modern science. As the late Willis Harman, Ph.D. pointed out in his book *Global Mind Change* (Warner Books), the past century has made it possible for us to exert an unprecedented influence on nature, fending off the dark with electric lights, taming bacteria with antibiotics. It is this—the ability to apply external solutions to what, in previous centuries, forced us to come to terms with awesome forces beyond our control or understanding—that has supported the illusion that we are just on the verge of having it all.

In the scientific era, so many of the "miracles" we once thought to be beyond rational understanding have been replicated on demand. Microscopic cameras probe the inner struggles of a single sperm as it navigates upstream towards a waiting egg on prime-time educational television. Skeletons are uncovered from the earth's deep stratas, filling in the gaps concerning our species' history. We are faced with discrepancies between scientific information and our religious beliefs. Usually, science wins. If we just work hard enough, we can figure out a way to call the shots in relation to whatever's bothering us. No need for miracles drawn from the irrational realm of religion and spirituality. Like young children, we put our super-hero capes over our pinstriped suits, stamp our feet, and proclaim to the universe, "I can do it by myself." The best minds in the world are at work solving whatever riddles yet remain. And as our scientists set themselves to the task of discovering the secrets of life, so our businesspeople put themselves to the task of wrenching personal success out of the economy.

Our ancestors did not have this certainty about their abilities to determine their destinies. For all the plagues and pestilence, devoid of rational explanation, each individual knew that his or her only hope was to call some kind of truce with the universe. We, whose inheritance has been the western rational mind, live in a world of expanded choices. We have religious freedom, a democratic system of government, upward and downward mobility, liberation of race and of gender. The freedom we have relinquished is our right to set aside logic and allow our hearts to take a leap of faith.

Where our forebearers called upon divine guidance to help make sense of the things that happened to them, we have consumerism offering us the promise of a better life. Our ancestors were forced to learn humility before an unpredictable universe. Yet today, when things begin to spin out of our control, our first impulse is to buy, add, or change something that promises to, at the very least, post-pone discomfort. As long as fate allows, we choose to believe that there is no problem or pain so serious that it can't be relieved by a new job, a new employee, a new piece of equipment, a raise. Our economy depends on us to add more "things" to our lives. We try everything we can think of to avoid disappointment.

A growing number of us have discovered that in the race to the finish line, we have large gaps in our understanding about life. We have learned how to make some money—or, at the very least, how to juggle lines of credit. We have learned how to start and raise families. Some of us have even taken great strides towards making contributions to society through community involvement. But we have not yet begun to understand what it takes to grasp the meaning of our lives.

Why? The program is flawed.

The programming we use teaches us that we can judge ourselves and others on the basis of one's ability to avoid discomfort. We invest energy trying to control reality, altering the circumstances with which we are faced. But if we believe we are rewarded for how good we are, then when things go wrong—as, sooner or later, they inevitably do—it must be our fault. We, who are so willing to be held accountable for our results, have only been prepared to win.

In the effort to grab the Golden Fleece of success, we throw everything we've got into our worklives. The more we put into them, the more complex and demanding the management problems we face become. As fast as our salaries and companies grow, our expenses and overhead grow faster.

This happened to one of The Orsborn Company's consultants, a small law practice that decided that the way to success was to take big, glamorous space in the top building in the downtown financial district. To justify the space, they added staff. To pay for the overhead, they raised their fees. Within six months, the lawyers had alienated their client base by assigning new associates to the work while charging higher prices. In the end, they only got one major assignment: doing the paperwork on their own dissolution.

Before long, the drive for "more" transforms from straight-ahead ambition fueled by the drive for control, to the convoluted compulsion to shore up the breaches in the structure at all costs. When you reach this critical stage, you may truly believe that your best hope is to stay so busy you don't have the time to admit you have already bitten off more than you can chew.

Melinda started a small business, offering fashion advice and shopping services for busy executives in her town. Melinda loved shopping and had great fashion sense. This seemed like the ideal career for her. For one year, she contented herself serving a loyal group of customers. Just busy enough, she was usually available to them when they needed a consultation. But charging on an hourly basis, her profits eventually plateaued. She began to think about expanding her services.

One of her customers approached her about a multi-level marketing opportunity, ostensibly selling vitamins and nutritional supplements. The real money, however, came from finding subordinate associates to come into the business who would both sell product and bring in yet other associates. Melinda saw this as a great opportunity to expand. At first, she started slow. When her clients called for a fashion consultation, she took the opportunity to try to sell them on getting involved in the vitamin business. This alienated most of her clients who might listen politely and order a bottle of vitamin C's, but avoid Melinda in the future. As her business dropped off, she became frantic seeking out prospects for the vitamin business, now not only to raise the plateau—but to make up for lost income. The more time she spent working the field, trolling her roster of acquaintances for prospects, the less available she was to her once loyal customers. Before long, trying to sell others on the vitamin business was no longer a supplement to her core service. It had taken over her life. People rarely came to her for fashion or shopping consultations. All of her friends and acquaintances—down to the dentist and the shoemaker—dreaded her calls and visits. The harder she worked, the further away from the fulfillment of both her personal and professional goals she found herself. Finally, Melinda decided to start over again, going back to her original business as a fashion consultant. She gave up her monetary-based definition of success, admitting that she loved her work and the freedom it afforded her. So what if she couldn't trade up her Saturn for a Lexus? This time, she would set a new goal for herself: to be happy with just enough.

No wonder we become afraid. We believe we are on the track that will take us the fastest way possible to the achievement of our goals, and the ground crumbles beneath our feet with every step. We are scared of not having enough, scared of demanding bosses, of losing clients, losing jobs, falling behind.

Ironically, it is fear itself that is the richest breeding ground for inferior performance. Who is at their best when fear is calling the shots? Where are creativity and vitality? Where is self-confidence, encouraging the taking of risks? Where is authenticity—the willingness to speak honestly and take the consequences? When you are driven by fear, you judge yourself, those who report to you, and the world around you harshly. You fear receiving from others what fear drives you to dish out.

"Like all people, managers behave according to their assumptions of how the world works—whether, for instance, it is a kind or a cruel place. Disastrous behavior follows when a manager's assumptions about the world establish a dangerous and self-defeating pattern," explains Professor Louis B. Barnes, D.B.A., of Harvard University Business School, an early supporter of these principles. "Obeying a distorted golden rule, people do to others what they perceive is being done to them."

So twisted have circumstances become that in some industries, individuals are praised for stealing product ideas, business relationships, and marketing opportunities. Ripping off your employer, even someone who has mentored and nurtured you, to form the basis for one's own competitive new venture is often perceived as resourceful. (Until, of course, one of the hot shots in your new company turns around and does the same thing to you.) If you get caught at unethical practices, a large enough contribution to the right kind of charity can buy back the appearance of respectability.

When you play the game of success by gathering as much power as possible for yourself in a fear-driven environment, you put your subordinates and coworkers on the defensive. Everyone is considered guilty until proven innocent. As a result, our organizations run along brittle, authoritarian lines as individuals battle each other for control.

Faced with accusatory tones, we have to wade through feelings of personal inadequacy, mounting an internal defense, before we can respond to even the most basic questions.

"Where's the report you promised me?"

"Why haven't you delivered those results?"

When faced with negative expectations, people spend a good percentage of time reacting to real or implied threats. They find themselves spending more time reporting on what they are doing and less time getting work done. More time is spent in meetings trying to "share" responsibility (and avoid taking blame.) Precious creative energy is wasted processing the tumultuous emotions, instead expressing itself as resentment.

When you are forced to operate out of fear, you shut out perspective and insight. Squelching intuition, you are forced to do everything the hard way. Devoid of inspiration, you resort to faking excellence. When an anxious client or boss is breathing down your neck, you are more likely to put on a show of hard work. You will call every prospect on your long lists to hit one who will say yes. The tone of desperation and resentment makes even that one a tough sell.

In a more supportive environment, you would be more likely to look over the larger list of contacts and intuitively know how to choose those few calls to make that will garner the same or, more likely, superior results. When you connect, you are relaxed and effective. You complete your day at work whole and healthy, rather than reactive and depleted.

Operating out of fear of abusive authority and competition is exhausting enough. But the real battle—the struggle that sets the stage for the enactment of the external drama—is internal. Sooner or later, each one of us must confront the even bigger conflict that is inside ourselves. In your struggle to make a living, you may be driven by the hope that your frantic efforts to make a big enough success of yourself will be sufficient to eradicate any possibility of pain. But you are sooner or later confronted with something unavoidable, seeping in through your armor's cracks: the disillusionment that comes when you realize that your effort to avoid pain through success at work is doomed.

Which player will win out? The self-delusion that your frantic efforts to keep control will do the trick—or disillusionment? In our society, disillusionment is the more terrifying prospect because when you surrender the childlike belief that you can control the world by being good enough, there is nothing waiting in the wings to take its place.

In our consumer-driven society, precious few of our spiritual institutions are willing to burst our illusions and provide us with something that will truly nurture our spirits. Many of our religious leaders have become packagers of the kind of experiences we think we want, rather than challenging us to painful but potentially more fruitful possibilities. Meditations in some religious institutions are ninety seconds or less—and even these truncated moments of contemplation are given a backdrop of easy-listening organ and choir, complete with a soprano who sings aloud for us what we wished our own hearts were feeling. Some religious institutions market themselves on the basis of their sports facilities and catering. Needing big-time contributions to keep the congregations competitive with shopping centers and entertainment parks, religious organizations are often run on the same principles of power and money operative in the world beyond the sanctuary walls.

Seeking guidance outside of organized religion, you may be pandered to by the superficial on one hand. But on the other hand, seek out spiritual teachers who have the potential to awaken the untapped powers of your heart, and you may find that you have opened yourself to the unscrupulous, the fraudulent, and the power-hungry. Many so-called awakeners cross the line between empowering people and exploiting them. You are on dangerous turf when you are asked to go out and recruit new followers as evidence and practice of your expanding mastery of life. Take care if you are promised perfect happiness and control. Watch out if questioning your guide is perceived as disloyalty. Eschew wisemen and women who teach one thing but do another.

Even if the biggest risk you take is to read this book, you may have to grapple with the question: How do I surrender to forces beyond my control without losing myself in the process? The only thing stronger than your desire to take a leap of faith to a life that has meaning is the fear that you will be let down again. Over and over again you will dismiss your search for meaning, asking yourself if there really is something better for you than battling to gain control? As much as you have already given, isn't this just a matter requiring more self-discipline, more willpower, more effort?

Give in to these impulses and you will find yourself running even faster, chased through worlds of ambition by fear.

Or, as this principle teaches, you can try something new.

What can you do to break the deadlock?

You, who pride yourself on your ability to do it by yourself, will not like the answer.

Accept irresolution.

Accept restlessness, insecurity, and pain.

Let the great internal battles rage! Should you push ahead? Quit? Struggle for meaning? Surrender to meaninglessness?

There is a reality external to yourself over which you have no control. Every choice contains risk. You cannot embark on the path that will lead you to an experience of true success until you confront the fact that work is tough and you can't always do something about it.

Is this depressing, or is this—as the Principles of Inner Excellence contend—liberating? It is not the fact that work is tough that stops you from experiencing success. Ironically, it is the degree to which fear of admitting that you don't have perfect control motivates your life that your businesses and careers will suffer. Unless you are willing to face the fact that you can never be good enough to fix everything that happens to you, the opportunity to live life fully will elude you. You will be too busy running away from the truth, throwing your how-to books with their false promises of easy success into the bonfire of your deeper suspicions that you are destined to have problems. If you suppress internal conflict, opting for busy, acquisitive responses to internal drives, you will be condemned to an ultimately unfulfilling existence.

It is your fundamental human right to have a trusting relationship with the universe that makes sense of your life. This longing for faith in something greater than yourself is legitimate. Just as you have physical needs for sufficient sleep and food, you have spiritual needs that you desire to have fulfilled. When you lose your connection to faith, you become angry at yourself for your restlessness—angry at your spiritual hunger. You try to blot out irresolution, squelching your yearning for a life that has meaning. You give up your ideals, compromise your integrity—hoping that more power will bring you the peace you seek. You take your frustration out on your employees, fellow workers, or your family. You get busy or ambitious, drugged or drunk, dulling the pain for as long as you can.

If you suppress the yearning, you are doomed to be at the mercy of the pervasive beliefs that unconsciously shape every aspect of how you run your career.

The first step of the journey to inner excellence requires that you neither deny your pain nor try to control it by changing others, your situation, or yourself. You must find it in you to sit patiently with complexity and imperfection without feeling compelled to find superficial, premature resolution.

Many of you will not have the courage to go this route until you've exhausted every other possibility. But only by surrendering your illusion of control can you hope to escape the destructive urges that drive your ambition.

Affirmation

I surrender the illusion that I can control everything that happens to me and to those I care about.

Principle Number Two

In order to become fully successful, you must first be fully alive.

———•◦•———

*W*hen you surrender the illusion of control, there is only one way left to find fulfillment: by cultivating an appreciation for the full range of creativity and destruction that life contains. You cannot be fully successful unless you are first fully alive.

What do I mean when I say "fully alive?" We all know people who are faced with challenges. Some fold under the pressure. Others thrive. Resilient people—the ones who emerge from setbacks in their careers, businesses, and lives with their vitality intact—understand that it is out of the nurturing of their characters and spirits that new possibilities will most readily arise.

When you give up your life-sapping efforts to control everything that happens to you, you experience everything from ecstasy to despair. You submit to uncertainty and confusion. The key is to give up resistance and accept where you are right now, no matter how uncomfortable that place may be. Our characters and spirits thrive on honesty and truth. It doesn't have to feel good to be growth. In fact, there is no safety in being fully alive—no guarantees that you will get through unscathed. This

Second Principle of Inner Excellence asks you to sacrifice the illusion of safety for the realization of what it means to be awake and alive.

Joy, sorrow, success, failure—all of life is creativity and destruction. The forces of nature are constantly creating and destroying to make way for new growth. Forest fires burn away the underbrush so that deeper roots can be nourished with life-giving light and water. Pine cones burst open in the heat, releasing their seeds to create new life. So it is when you are fully alive. When faced with challenges, you let go of what you have, opening the space for new possibilities to come to you. Rather than use your vital energy to protect what you fear losing, you have your full energy available to you to attract even greater opportunities for yourself. This very process of making space, this process of discovery, inspires you to release your old beliefs—your old ways of doing things—to embrace new ways that will be better for you. This is what it truly means to fulfill your human potential—not to try to make the forced attempt to limit yourself to living your life on the narrow band most people think of as "happiness," but rather to expand to embrace the entire range of human emotions.

The misguided attempt to protect yourself from pain may have come quietly, such as when you decide not to say to another what you really feel. When you keep busy in order to avoid your feelings. When you don't do what you know is right because you don't know why you should bother. When you show off to impress others.

After many years as a hairdresser in somebody else's shop, Brian, an acquaintance of mine, decided to fulfill his lifelong dream of opening his own salon. Hoping to guarantee himself a successful business, he plotted and planned the best salon he could imagine—something far greater than what he had previously experienced. While his track record was built on his warm rapport with his clients and fellow hairdressers, Brian dismissed his way of doing business as "small-time." His new salon would be the next "in spot," the kind of place people would wait three months for a haircut.

In recruiting hairstylists for his shop, Brian passed up many of his friends, renting booth space instead to flashy stylists lured from other salons he perceived as more successful. Brian's strategy turned out to be a disaster. Many of the stylists he brought in looked great, yet were rude and arrogant not only to him, but to their clients. His client base began to turn over, the losses outpacing the gains. Devoid of an established base of loyalty, many of the new associates considered Brian's salon to be a stepping stone rather than a home. Soon there were empty chairs throughout the shop.

In desperation, Brian reached out to his former friends. It was hard to do, but he finally admitted that in his effort to avoid the pain of failure, he had marched straight ahead into its jaws. He was wrong. He apologized, admitting that despite his big investment in cutting-edge decor and equipment, he hadn't a clue about how to make his salon the next trendy shop. All he knew was how to provide a place of nurturing, service, and enjoyment for the kind of people who were naturally attracted to his way of doing things. Beyond that, the chips would have to fall as they may.

Forgiving him, many of his friends joined up. The clients came back. Soon, Brian had one of the most successful (if not trendiest) shops in town.

The temptation is always to give up your authenticity in the pursuit of comfort. You go for what looks good, rather than listening to your own heart. You seek to take refuge in what you believe other people would call successful, rather than trusting your own way of doing things. Brian found that in the short-term, he could put together a trendy salon that would support the illusion of success. But before long, the weaknesses in the structure inevitably would take their toll.

The key to being fully alive is acceptance. Brian learned to trust his strengths and mourn his losses. At last, he faced the pain that he could not outwit fate by being trendy or clever enough. He gave up his attempt to build a successful shop on the narrow band we are taught to think of as "success." Rather, he expanded to embrace the broader complexities and potentialities of his life. Out of desperation, he chose to begin paying attention to the growth and nurturing of his character and spirit. Ironically, by surrendering to his limitations, Brian found the most direct path to success.

Another friend of mine, Marsha, was not so fortunate. Managing the retail operations of a bank, Marsha had by her side a trusted protégé, Carl. Over the years, she shared more and more power with her associate. In exchange for the power, he increasingly took on the unpleasant or painful tasks encountered in the normal course of doing business. If there was trouble with a subordinate, a supplier or outside consultants, Marsha assigned the hot spots to Carl. She prided herself on her ability to manage, given the relatively pain-free environment Carl created for her. But in the shadow of laziness disguised as delegation, she eventually became dependent on him. Unfortunately, she did not realize this until the day he came to her, explaining that he had received a competitive job offer and was planning to leave.

Despite the fact that Marsha had managed the retail operation brilliantly for the several years prior to hiring

Carl—including the difficult tasks she subsequently assigned to him—she was now willing to do whatever it took to keep him. She dreaded the threat of returning to the front lines, but she wouldn't admit this, even to herself. Instead, she justified her actions in the name of generosity, faith, and gratitude, dealing Carl most of her remaining power cards. She denied herself, her own competence, and her ability to keep herself from having to feel the pain of her responsibilities.

Carl stayed. But even while pledging his renewed allegiance to Marsha, Carl's outstanding work couldn't help but be recognized by the head of the bank. Eventually, when the opportunity presented itself, Carl was promoted over Marsha. Not long thereafter, Marsha left the bank.

By trying to protect herself, Marsha chose the very path that led her in the fastest and most direct way to the realization of her worst fears.

There is another way. My hairdresser friend Brian found it—and so can you.

One of my favorite stories shows us where to begin:

An engineer was checking construction on the top floor of a partially completed highrise. He slipped on a beam, saving himself temporarily from a precipitous fall by grabbing on to it. Hanging forty floors above street level, the engineer felt the beam begin to slip.

This man had never believed in God, but felt that this was as good a time as any to begin.

"God, are you up there?"

"Yes, my son," God replied. "What can I do for you?"

"God, help me. Tell me what to do!" he cried.

"You really want to know?"

The beam slipped a bit more.

Desperate, the engineer cried out again.

"Yes, God. Tell me!"

There was a moment's silence. Then God answered him.

"Let go of the beam."

"Let go of the beam?"

"Yes, my son. Let go of the beam."

There was another moment's silence, then the engineer spoke.

"Is there anybody else up there?"

You say you want success, the kind of success that will last? The price is steep. You have wasted so much precious time and energy operating under the pretense that you are in charge. Perhaps you, like the man holding onto the beam, believe you are fulfilling your potential when in truth, you are exhausting it. Spirit urges you to release over and over again old ways of working and living that are deadening to your spirit. You must be willing to tell the truth, to listen to your heart, to take risks. If you aspire to a life of meaning and purpose, I know of only one way that does not involve falling into the void. That is to climb down into it. Grab your flashlight and begin exploring. Are you fully alive? Take this simple test and you may realize why the experience of success you have tried so hard to achieve has eluded you.

1. Do you keep yourself so busy putting out fires you don't have time to think about the bigger picture?
2. Do you do things simply to win the approval of others, rather than doing them out of a true sense of giving of yourself?
3. Do you avoid doing what's right because it takes too much time or might bring you pain?
4. Do you put the accomplishments of others down, instead of appreciating your own?

5. Do you refrain from saying what you really feel to others because you hope to avoid unpleasantness, even when you know that to keep quiet lacks integrity?
6. Do you turn against yourself or others when anything goes wrong?
7. Are you willing to take risks—but only if you know things will turn out for you?

If you answered yes to any of these questions, you are still trying to maintain the illusion of control. Accept the pain of having to come face to face with your limitations. This won't be easy. Admitting helplessness is a last, desperate resort. But it is the only way to the experience of success for which you yearn. When you find the courage to let go of your illusions, you are forced to confront the alternative: Some degree of suffering is the inevitable fallout of being human. Only when you are willing to let go of your precarious perch do you free yourself from enslavement to the defense of your illusions. This is quite simply not your show. What a relief!

The most successful real estate investor I know is one who specializes in renovating difficult properties. Before concluding his deals, he goes through the troubled buildings with qualified contractors. He catalogs all the problem areas. Even so, he assumes that no matter how careful he is, after the closing, more will be discovered.

When new problems arise, he feels relieved. His reasoning: He has learned that in anything worthwhile, there are going to be problems. He looks forward to hearing what they are. At least then he knows which problems he's going to be dealing with. The faster he finds out what is wrong, the faster he can correct and move on. While others I know have shipwrecked on the shoals of real estate investing, complaining about how they took a hit on this or that deal, vowing to avoid any of these problems by finding a better deal the next time out, our friend has built a multimillion dollar real estate empire on their rejects.

When you stop wasting energy repressing negative possibilities, you have your complete potential available to you. I learned this lesson one challenging Fourth of July weekend. The plan was that following one last routine client meeting, I would meet my family at the swimming pool of a local resort for an afternoon of fun and sun. Little did I suspect that this meeting would include a pink slip, notifying me that our agency's services were being terminated. Stumbling out of their office, lost in a fog of remorse, I missed the turn-off to the resort. By the time I came to, I was an hour's drive farther from my holiday than where I'd started. The long drive back to my family was accompanied by the increasing determination that not only did this failure signify that the business was doomed—but that I was the one killing it.

At last I arrived at the resort, crawling to the pool in utter despair. After hearing my sad story, Dan offered his assurance of faith in me and the business we had built together. The children urged me to join them for a frolic in the pool.

I was immobilized. Doomed to failure. How could I ever find my way out of the abyss?

Then, I had a tiny, new thought.

What if I could be in despair—and in the pool at the same time?

I found an out-of-the-way step where I could soak and sulk simultaneously. Then Grant came by and splashed me on the leg. I brushed him away. Not long thereafter, Grant and Jody came, squealing with delight as they churned the warm water around my step. I asked them to give me space. Then Dan joined them. Before long, my family had engaged me in a splashing contest. Despite myself, the despair could not survive the onslaught of love and laughter.

Surrender came when I understood that, whether my destiny was to succeed or fail in the business, it would come not from squashing or punishing myself, but from being more of who and what I am at any moment. This includes despair as well as joy, moments of genius as well as flat-out failure. I had to trust that my greatest success would come not from undermining my spirit, but rather, from nurturing it. Surrendering to the embrace of the greater range of the full human potential — being willing to hold it all at the same time — this is the secret of resilient people, and the only path to inner excellence.

Affirmation

I am willing to embrace all that I am — including my fears, pain, and limitations as well as my loves, comforts, and happiness — realizing that in doing so, I am expanding to fulfill my true human potential.

Principle Number Three

When you give up the illusion of who you thought you were, there is less to lose than you had feared.

———◦———

The degree to which you stop protecting yourself from unpleasant possibilities, emotions, and information is the degree to which you can deal with what is real.

Jeremy, one of my former clients, runs a nonprofit organization dedicated to bringing peace to the world. He can rage eloquently about his desire for world leaders to learn to listen—while not allowing anyone in his presence to get a word in edgewise. He can rally for toleration of dissent in the world while exiling his own dissident staff members to organizational Siberia. Everyone who knows this man admires his results. Few admire his tactics. What energy he must invest in every moment of every day to avoid recognizing in himself the very qualities he has devoted his life to eliminating in the world!

Can you recognize how much of your career and life are dominated by your desire to avoid seeing things about yourself that are most obvious to others?

Dan and I stumbled onto this uncomfortable inner terrain in the form of a half-eaten coffee cake. The cake made its fateful appearance on our conference room table early one morning at a time when we appeared to be at the height of our success as an agency. We had just won our industry's highest award, a Silver Anvil. Our staff had grown to more than twenty people. Despite the foreboding I'd felt upon signing the mortgage papers to our dream house, we were still living the fast-track lifestyle, looking to all the world like we had it all.

Each and every day, Dan and I led the charge, working seventy or more hours a week, expecting our team to do the same. We worked nights. They worked nights. We worked weekends. They worked weekends.

Every week at our staff meeting, Dan and I produced a self-congratulatory coffee cake for our hard-charging, award-winning team, setting it on the table while regaling them with stories designed to motivate and inspire. The staff would shake their heads, applaud, laugh, and nibble.

Thus bonded, we would set them loose to work even harder and longer, setting greater goals, scaling ever grander heights of heady success.

But our weekly staff meeting was held in the afternoon. And this was morning.

And this was not our coffee cake.

When we finally mustered the courage to launch an inquiry, our most senior staff member explained that there was growing discontent among the troops. They had gotten together without us—exhausted and resentful—to let off steam.

But what about our staff meetings? Wasn't that their opportunity to tell us how they felt? Week after week, we had watched them bond in teamwork, invigorated by our inspired leadership to set and achieve bigger and better goals.

Our staff member looked away sadly, then took a big breath, gathering courage to proceed.

"Dan, Carol," he said, "your stories are very inspiring. But that's not why we nod, laugh, and applaud."

"It's not?" We breathed deeply, gathering courage to respond. "Then why do you do it?"

"We listen to your stories, then do what you ask us to do because we are afraid of losing our jobs."

At that moment, we had a choice to make. We could have invalidated our senior staff person's evaluation. We could have fired him, and the whole staff for that matter. At the same time, we could have ignored the coffee cake and tried to forget the whole thing.

Or we could stop and sneak a peek into the old, dusty, padlocked box that was the place we were most reluctant to look: to see through the illusion of our office camaraderie—our brilliant leadership. Ironically, we were being told that we only thought we were inspiring our staff when, in actuality, we were terrifying them. Was there truth in what was being said about us? The queasy response in our stomachs—and the urge to run away—were indications that there was, indeed, a discrepancy between who we thought we were and how we were actually perceived. We could not swallow this all in one gulp. But on that fateful day, we became willing to see the bigger picture, including the part we had played, more clearly. Only when we had a better grasp on reality could we make the corrections that would bring our company and lives back into alignment with our highest aspirations: to make a living not despite our characters and spirits, but because of them. This was the initiation of the process of inner excellence in earnest: the reevaluation of assumptions we'd taken for granted all of our lives and the subsequent changes that would have to be made in ourselves and our company.

What we discovered is this: When you let glimpses of the truth seep between the cracks of your preferred version of reality, you begin to experience the most exquisite pain. Your old constructions may fall apart as the foundation that no longer works for you begins to crumble. Do you grab on—or do you let the old ways go, trusting that you have the right to a life built on the solid ground of authenticity, not the sands of delusion? The truth is that we didn't lose control over our company because our employees chose to meet in secret to express their frustration. We had lost control of our staff long before that coffee cake ever hit the table. Choosing to ignore all the hints and signs that something was amiss, we had built our success on unstable ground. We so hate to give up our precious fantasies. Even if we suspect that something's missing or wrong, we prefer to pump ourselves up, slick things over, and postpone our moment of reckoning as long as possible. Do you have the courage to see what is really going on in your job, career, or business—early on, when it will be less painful for you to make the corrections? Try to avoid the pain entirely, and you will find yourself—as were we—engulfed in an even bigger crisis. The task seems enormous. Where should you begin?

A classic story from the Zen tradition gives us a place to start:

Once upon a time, a young seeker went in search of a spiritual teacher. He travelled across India to find himself at last at the door of a master, who invited him in for a cup of tea. Seated at the table, the boy extolled his qualifications for disciplehood: his hard work, his accomplishments, his self-discipline, and his studies. As he talked, the master poured a cup of tea out of a large pot. The boy noticed that the cup was nearly full. Then, the tea began spilling over the cup onto the saucer.

As he continued talking, the boy realized that the master had filled the cup so full, it was now overflowing onto the table and into his lap.

"Master!" the boy exclaimed. "You're spilling the tea!"

The master smiled, and told the boy, "You are like this cup of tea! So full, there's room for no more. Come to me empty, then we can begin."

I was once interviewed by Marina, a new business writer for a regional newspaper, concerning the Seven Principles of Inner Excellence. After her deadline, she called to tell me how the story of the disciple and the master had helped her turn an important corner professionally.

Marina explained to me that, recently hired as a "self-starter," she was still needing to prove herself to her editor. At the same time, she knew that many of her readers would think that "inner excellence" belonged on the religion rather than the business page. Concerned about appearing foolish, she had filled a wastebasket with false starts.

"I hadn't wanted to admit that I was having trouble. After all, I really thought I was a hot shot landing this job. But after rereading the story about the disciple, I realized that I didn't need to pretend to be an ace reporter when what I really am is a beginner. This was clearly a case where I could go and ask for help from my editor."

As a result, the managing editor had not only offered her the help she sought, but had given her a compliment.

"One of the reasons I hired you over the other applicants is that I thought I could trust you to know what you know—and know what you don't know. I'd much rather

you come to me for help when you need it than to turn out
a poorly-conceived article."

You think you will get ahead faster if you are, like the
overflowing teacup, "full of yourself." But given that you
invest so much energy selling people on yourself, why is it
that so many people don't seem to "get" you?

The authority figures in your early years passed
along to you coping strategies drawn from their experience of life. Coming of age in anxious times, your parents undoubtedly were doing their best to help you nav-
igate the dangerous reefs of survival. The messages many
of us got—however loving our parents' motivation—
were the product of generations of fear. The result is that
our natural faith and optimism—our authentic percep-
tions and inclinations—were invalidated over and over
again and replaced with principles supplied by outside
authorities.

Every family has its own secret set of beliefs, going
back through many generations. Perhaps some on this list
of commonly held beliefs will be familiar, but your list will
be uniquely yours. You were taught from birth to swim in
your parents' own particular color water. Your acceptance
into your first community—upon which your early survival depended—required that you adopt the beliefs as
your own. In previous chapters, you already explored one
of the deep-seated beliefs that you were saddled with from
early childhood: "Be good and you will be rewarded." But
there are many, many others.

In a fear-driven culture, you may be honored by your
community for the adoption of qualities that are, in reality, the result of obsolete, potentially destructive patterns:
for example, the gymnastics coach who is celebrated for
his selfless generosity while in truth he is exploiting young
talent to enhance his own reputation, or the assistant

admired for her faithfulness who covers up her boss's drinking to increase his dependency upon her.

Do any of these fear-based beliefs sound familiar to you?

- Don't trust other people.
- Imperfection is a sign of weakness.
- Introspection is self-indulgent.
- Asserting divergent desires is disloyal.
- If you want to get ahead, don't rock the boat.
- To get the job done right, you have to do it yourself.
- You will only be loved if you deny your own needs to please others.
- Don't speak the truth if it might disturb somebody.

What if your early survival was dependent on adopting beliefs that, in the long run, are destructive to you?

My friend Hal, a production manager employed by a direct mail fashion cataloger, was an excellent employee who anticipated what was needed of him and performed consistently beyond expectations. But Hal had some concerns about certain corporate practices that he decided to keep to himself. Because he believed that if you want to get ahead, don't rock the boat, he was sure that if he expressed his concerns, he would not be viewed as a team player and would be passed over for promotion. When an opportunity for advancement opened up, the company shocked Hal by announcing that it was going outside the organization to search for someone who could bring new ideas to the business—precisely what Hal had been holding back. At this point, what did Hal have to lose? Taking a deep breath, he took the risk of telling his boss his honest opinions. The boss was silent for a long moment. Then, at last, he spoke.

"I had no idea you were thinking about these things. That's just the kind of feedback we're looking for."

Hal got the promotion.

Here's another example of how our beliefs can play out in the workplace. I became friendly with Donna, the personnel director of one of our client companies, an insurance group headquartered on the west coast. A dedicated career woman, Donna believed that if she missed one single day, the company would fall apart. "If you want it done right, you've got to do it yourself," was her favorite saying. She worked nights, weekends, easily seventy or eighty hours a week. She often complained about her long hours and felt that she was on the verge of a physical and emotional breakdown.

Then she got pregnant. The woman who never took a day for herself developed a problem pregnancy that required bed rest—for a month! Suddenly, Donna had to rearrange her entire worklife, bringing home the essential parts of her job she could do in bed via phone and computer. The rest she was forced to trust to her staff. Excited by the opportunity to show their stuff, the staff pulled together and produced superior work. Ironically, by over-controlling the situation, all Donna had accomplished in all those years of hard work was the squashing of her staff's spirit and the advancement of her own exhaustion. After the baby was born, Donna returned to work, but she did not resume her marathon work schedule. Realizing that she did not have to be a one-woman band, she continued to experiment with teamwork and delegation. By simply changing her beliefs, she was able to cut her work week as much as fifty percent! She had the time she needed to take care of herself and her new baby girl.

"If you want it done right, you've got to do it yourself" is one belief she hopefully won't be passing along to her daughter.

Kirk is another businessperson who, like Donna, had been suffering needlessly for far too long because of his beliefs. Kirk was referred to me by the head of the Nashville office of one of the country's largest corporate outplacement firms to supplement their extensive counseling and placement services with something new to the field: spiritual guidance. My friend explained to me that Kirk had come to the city to take a top job in a healthcare company. Less than three months after his relocation, the company unexpectedly shut its doors. Kirk had gone out on a number of exploratory interviews with other healthcare providers in the area, but nobody was hiring at his level. Kirk had gone through a whole range of emotions, from angry to sad, from scared to bitter. He'd always thought of himself as a spiritual person, but suddenly he felt himself to have been left alone to fend for himself in a hostile universe.

Kirk realized both intellectually and emotionally how much better it would be if he could reinvigorate his faith in life. He remembered that when he felt good about himself, he approached new people and situations with confidence. Driven by inspiration rather than fear, his vitality naturally attracted opportunities. He read several books about affirmations and positive thinking. But even if his intellectual powers understood how important such a return to faith would be, the blow his ego had suffered had undermined his capacity to remain optimistic. His faith, it appeared, had turned out to be a fair-weather friend: active and vital when things were going his way, but fleeing into the dark night the moment something went wrong.

"I want my faith back, but it doesn't work for me to tell myself that this is a loving universe. I've tried that—positive thinking—and I feel like a fake. If it's not real for me, I just can't do it. How can someone like me go about reversing destructive beliefs while staying true to myself?"

As Kirk suspected, growing spiritually is not simply a matter of replacing a negative thought with a positive one. The spiritual path is not about applying superficial resolution or escape to obtain temporary relief from one's problems. It is, rather, the path for people who want to be more fully alive. On the spiritual path, pain is not the problem—but the point of entry to a deeper, more fulfilling life.

In the Jewish tradition, the individual who is willing to engage in this level of participation is called a *tzaddik*, a righteous leader. Dissatisfaction is the emotional state that lets the tzaddik know when it is time to make a new effort at advancement. To stay at one's current spiritual level, regardless of how exalted it might be, is considered to be a sin.

Kirk would evolve through his pain. His character and spirit would strengthen as a result of his spiritual journey. But in the meantime, he needed a job. How could he find a spiritual place from which to act that would not be faked or forced?

"Kirk, are you sure that you've been abandoned? Or is it possible that this is your fear?"

"Well, I certainly fear it—but that doesn't mean it isn't true. Maybe the universe has abandoned me."

"Maybe so. But then again, maybe it hasn't. You see, the thing is, when we give up control in our lives, the first thing we realize is that we can't always stop the bad things from happening to us."

"Is there a second thing?" he asked.

"Simply this: You can't stop the good things from happening, either. You have to admit that it is just as possible for the best outcome to transpire as the worst. The thing is, you can't always make the good things happen. But at least you can stop blocking their way."

"How?"

"Make room for them by clearing away your outmoded beliefs."

"Oh, positive thinking. But I already told you, I can't fake it."

"I'm not asking you to fake it. In fact, the only honest place to begin is exactly where you are right now. So, you yourself just told me that you cannot know for sure whether the universe has, in truth, abandoned you or not. Correct?"

Kirk paused for a moment to consider my question, then nodded affirmatively. I continued.

"The one thing you are certain of is that you are afraid you've been abandoned."

"Right."

"Then let's start with your fear."

Kirk and I bent over a yellow pad to work out some possible new programming that could help release the grip of the destructive beliefs that had taken hold of his worklife, and invite in something better for him.

Here's the steps we followed:

1. Identify a negative belief that is currently operating in your life.

   In Kirk's case, the pervasive belief was: "I have been abandoned to a hostile universe."

2. Voice an alternate possibility.

   Try flipping your destructive belief upside down. Kirk chose these words: "I am taken care of in a loving universe."

3. Put the two thoughts together.

   At first, all Kirk was willing to say was this: "Even though I fear I have been abandoned to a hostile universe, I am willing to consider the possibility that I am being taken care of in a loving universe."

4. Feel the emotions that arise.

Rather than use positive thinking to drown out his pain, Kirk decided to put everything he had—even his pain—into his affirmations. The words he wrote in his journal and repeated to himself daily were not magical incantations, but rather a spiritual tool engaging him in a process of growth. By following the steps, he became clear about the discrepancies between what was true for him now—and how he wished things really were. He didn't suppress the pain that arose from the discrepancies; rather, he felt his discomfort fully and acknowledged his progress as the discrepancies receded.

Through months of transition, Kirk continued to confront his fears and hold open the possibility of the return of his faith. At times, he felt crazy and upset. Sometimes, he felt like a teenager again, his feelings running away with him. The wall of outmoded beliefs he had erected in childhood to protect himself was crumbling due to the force of his own growth, and it was painful. Sometimes he asked himself if he was digging too deep. "Am I cracking through to someplace wonderful—or just cracking up?"

And yet, in the midst of the darkness, there was a small, still voice reminding him that life is not a skill to be mastered, but an adventure to be lived. Faith takes this into consideration; choosing to believe that however you are feeling at any given moment, the most optimistic outcome is still possible. Many influences will contribute to the resolution of the issues you face, and your very hope becomes one of those determining factors. Perhaps it is but a small consideration; but even so, it may carry just enough weight to make the difference.

Kirk stayed with it. For months, every time he felt abandoned by the universe, he pulled out his new journal book and wrote down his affirmation and the feelings that came bundled with it. As he went, he tested his boundaries, seeing how far he was willing to push his beliefs, editing as he went. Eventually, he summarized his progress by using the affirmation, "Good happens, too." In the process of working with his affirmation, Kirk was willing to meet himself in despair—and take baby steps back in the direction of hope. Indeed, it had taken faith to be willing to engage in the affirmation process in the first place.

Kirk began to feel more optimistic about the future. He volunteered for an important committee position with a prestigious nonprofit organization in the healthcare industry. He met people who could help him in a relaxed setting. When at last a call came for him to interview at a place he truly wanted to work, his spirit was intact rather than depleted. And he had a bonus: a new relationship to faith that he could count on in bad times as well as good. In fact, the experiences he went through while unemployed helped to build the exact skills and strengths he needed to call upon as one of the top healthcare executives in the city.

If it hadn't been for Kirk's dismissal from his job and Donna's problem pregnancy, forcing her to take time off, these two businesspeople may have continued to operate out of fear-driven beliefs for the durations of their work-lives. They may have missed the richness of the journey to the fully-lived life. They might never have suspected what they were missing. In fact, destructive beliefs—programmed in from birth—can come to feel safe, familiar, and comfortable to you. Try to put healthy beliefs in their place, think for yourself, and you may even find yourself burdened by troubled questions. Do you feel silly about your desire for faith? Does your longing for integrity seem self-indulgent? Does your desire to give and receive love seem counterproductive? Your reluctance to crack open this secret box is understandable. As destructive and fear-driven as the beliefs from which you've been operating your life have been, they accomplished their goal. What is that? Survival of the status quo. How do you know they worked? Because the very fact that you exist proves it. Step out of destructive programming to go with new beliefs and what will happen when things get tough? You worry that although the status quo may not be all that great, if you try something new, things could get even worse. Are you the kind of person who is truly willing to take the risk of being fully alive? Or would you prefer to continue to take refuge in your childlike hope that you are still in control?

What do you really want?

The answer lies deeply hidden in the places you are least likely to look: the places where you are ashamed, humiliated, or embarassed; where you are brittle and defensive; where you have accused others, fixating on the very qualities in those around you that you most fear finding in yourself. We fear disillusionment. But as painful as it is to become disabused from one's illusions, at least then you can begin to deal with what is real. One of my mentors, Lynn Lumbard, put it this way:

"Rather than working to expand your comfort level, work to expand your discomfort level."

Discomfort, yes. But how about flat-out pain?

Few of us choose pain. But more and more of us are choosing growth through an expanding awareness of ourselves, even knowing that pain may well be the fallout.

Why should you become willing to do anything that would bring pain on even if only as a by-product? Because the alternative is to be unpleasantly surprised over and over again by the damaging results of your unconsciously held assumptions and the resulting actions and reactions they engender daily in your life.

Jerry, one of our friends in the marketing business, thought he was a brilliant manager. However, Jerry couldn't keep a decent media buyer on staff. Several were fired because they made stupid mistakes. The competent ones always seemed to get job offers elsewhere that they couldn't refuse. Every time one left, our friend blamed the heated competition for experienced media buyers instead of considering whether or not he bore some responsibility. Only after a major snafu allowed his newest media buyer to commit to $100,000 of unauthorized television advertising for a client did our friend consider his role in the situation. The truth was that Jerry was a poor communicator, assuming that it was the media buyer's job to read his mind. Every time Jerry wrote a company check to the television station, gradually paying off the $100,000 debt, he wished he had learned his lesson when there had been less money at stake.

But there's more at stake than just money.

Do you want a relationship with the universe that makes sense of your life? Tell the truth about where you are, and you will have found the only place for you to begin. Ironically, it turns out that the very act of bringing your painful internal processes into the bright light of day can transform the very issues you have avoided confronting in yourself.

Open into the pain and hurt, and the wounds have the opportunity to heal. As incredible as this may sound, all you have to do to begin is to make yourself willing to see. The rest takes care of itself.

Until you have a sufficient data base to know this for yourself, you will need to act on faith. If things are hard for you right now, all the better! The illusions are already cracking and the ground shifting beneath your feet. In the void, the way things used to be release their grip and you have the freedom to try out new ways to live and work that will be healthier for you.

The remaining principles shared in this book build on the internal skills you are developing to have the experience of success you are seeking. At this point, it is necessary only to empty your teacup. You may sit before the empty cup feeling anxiety. Or you can sit before the empty cup feeling excitement.

All that matters is that your cup be empty. Empty of your illusions. Empty of the fantasy of control. Empty of old beliefs that no longer serve you. The path of inner excellence asks you to give up a lot. But look at the alternative: What if failure to control the things that happen to you was not the worst possibility? What if the greater tragedy was betrayal of your potential to live life fully?

Like the engineer hanging from the beam, you are already over the edge. What choice do you have?

Affirmation

I reclaim my right to authentic expression.

Principle Number Four

You have the choice between being victimized by circumstances or being initiated by them.

———•—————

*O*nce you realize that you are a beginner, you can let go of judging yourself solely on the basis of your results. Instead, you put your faith in the adventure of your life as it unfolds, regardless of your circumstances. Pay attention to the growth of your character and your spirit, and the rest will take care of itself.

The ancient Chinese philosopher Lao Tzu inspired his students with a simple story about a farmer and his horse:

Once there was a farmer whose only possession of merit was a prized horse. All the people in the village ridiculed the farmer.

"Why put all your money into a horse? Somebody could steal the horse and you will have nothing."

The horse did not get stolen. But sadly enough, the horse did run away.

"You fool. You should have diversified—not put so many eggs in one basket. Now you have nothing. You are so unlucky."

The farmer, being a wise man, answered:

"Don't say I'm unlucky. Just say that my horse is no longer here. This is a fact. We don't know what may happen next."

Sure enough, the next day the horse returned. And with him was a pack of wild stallions.

The villagers exclaimed, "You were so right! Look how fortunate you are!"

The farmer replied, "You cannot possibly know if this is fortunate or unfortunate. We do not have the whole story yet. Merely say that we have more horses than before."

The farmer set his only son to tame the wild horses. The son was thrown and broke his leg. The doctor said he would be crippled for life.

The villagers decried his misfortune but the farmer again asked them to withhold judgment.

Soon thereafter, a war broke out in their country and all the young, healthy sons were drafted into battle. Only the farmer's son was left behind. The fighting was fierce and most of the other boys in the village died at war.

"You were right again, farmer," they said.

The farmer shouted, "On and on you go, judging this, judging that. Who do you think you are? How is it that you can presume to know how this is all going to turn out in the end?"

Because you are not in position to judge the ultimate success or failure inherent in the things that happen to you, stop wasting valuable energy bribing fate with your manipulative behavior and get on with it.

When you have given what you can to any particular circumstance, do you get the result you think you want? Or do you let go to embrace instead whatever new directions and experiences circumstances bring to you? Are you able to reap your results now, or are they left to ripen on the vine for some future flowering beyond your expectations?

Over the years, we have known several extraordinary people who have refused to waste precious energy mourning lost opportunities. Joan opened a high-end toy store in downtown San Francisco, introducing new European toy lines to Americans. The market wasn't ready for the high-priced items. But one line of toys did better than most: miniature metal sports cars. As she was selling off her inventory, she decided to take a small ad in the *Wall Street Journal*. The response was astonishing! She had orders from all over the country. She couldn't close her store fast enough to start an Internet-based business selling the popular collectibles.

Another friend, Kent, had worked many years as a market research specialist with a bank in order to save enough money to open a small winery. All of us cheered him on as he took the leap toward fulfilling his dreams. Unfortunately, shortly thereafter—at a time when the whole wine industry was in trouble—his fledgling winery went bankrupt and Kent was out on the street with no prospects for starting up again. Would he have to go back to banking? Kent had pretty much given up hope until he had a brainstorm. He was now not only an expert on wine—but on bankruptcy. And who needed his services more now than wineries? As a market study specialist, Kent knew both the business challenges and emotional difficulties wineries were going through. He began to offer his services as an outside consultant, helping wine companies maximize whatever opportunities they had while guiding them to retreat gracefully should bankruptcy be their only choice.

When the wine industry recovered, Kent had a group of private investors approach him about getting his own winery going again. Surely he would jump at the chance to get back on track with his lifelong dream! Ironically,

Kent realized that what had at first appeared to be his misfortune had, in reality, given him the sense of purpose he'd been yearning for all of his life. Nobody was more surprised than he when he said no.

How many of us delay the opportunity to discover what could be next for us by getting stuck in the drama of the moment, thrashing about in the underbelly of our emotions. We are so quick to interpret feelings of fear, sadness, anger, or exhaustion as failure. We panic. We overreact. We turn on ourselves, our bosses, our employees, pointing bony fingers of blame and accusation every which way.

When interviewed by a sportswriter, the coach of a major league baseball team was asked to comment on the chances of bringing up a new, promising pitcher from the minors.

"There is plenty of talent in the minors," he commented. "In fact, some of the boys we have on the farm have stronger skills than the ones we've got here. But the thing is, it's not the talent that is the deciding factor in what makes a major league pitcher."

"What is?" asked the columnist.

"It's how well he learns to fail."

When I think of the successful people I've known over the years, I have to agree that it is their ability to fail—rather than their ability to produce a particular product or service—that has ultimately made the difference. When they come up on a problem, how fast do they let go of remorse to make the correction and move on? How quickly do they forgive themselves and find the courage to try again?

I spent an exhausting day going after new business for the agency, to no avail. That night, I got together with one of my friends who has always talked about going into business for herself. Instead, she opted for the security of a government job that bored her daily.

"I've had the worst day!" I shared with her over a round of sushi. "I've just spent the whole day on the phone being rejected."

I expected my friend to commiserate with me, reasserting the validity of her decision to remain in her safe haven. Instead, she looked at me with a surprising degree of envy.

"You've spent all day having people say no to you. But I've spent the whole day saying no to myself."

When you take the drama of self-punishment out of the process, you get to deal with a more objective view of the situation—not just what you fear may be your short-comings.

If there are corrections to be made, mistakes to be rectified, you will get to them quicker if you live your life as if what you do really matters. Spirituality is not passive. It takes great courage not to abandon yourself when life gets rough. That is what heroes discover about themselves as they face their dragons along the way. They must dig deep to find new levels of commitment, courage, and inspiration from which to draw.

Outside the business arena, what I fear most is snakes. Imagine my surprise when I took a week-long sabbatical from business, after a particularly exhausting bout with the agency's bottom line, to nurture myself in a meditative surrounding—only to be told that this year, for the first time in anybody's memory, the infamous green rattler, aptly nicknamed "seven seconds to heaven," had made its appearance within the retreat boundaries.

Through the weeks of doom and gloom that preceded this long-awaited retreat, I had sustained my efforts with the promise of contemplative hikes through the restorative mountain desert terrain and camping out under the stars. Instead, when my moment finally arrived, you would have found me—on those rare occasions I ventured outside the safety of my cabin—scurrying along the few paved paths between lodge and dining hall; or worse, frozen in terror as I attempted to discern whether the rattling sound was a cricket, a water sprinkler, or my last seven seconds.

After two or three days, scurrying about the desert chased by my terror, I realized that this was a surprisingly familiar feeling. Too familiar. Here it was snakes. At home, it was prospective clients who might not renew our contracts. Illness. Angry employees. Debts.

Then and there, I set my intention to go out into the desert as originally planned. I decided to spend a night on the mountain—from sunset to dawn, regardless of what might come along for me to face.

As I walked up the gentle slopes of the high desert foothills, I began my search for a place that felt welcoming and safe. Everywhere I looked, I saw things scurrying. Lizards, beetles, spiders. Forget snakes. I did my best not to think about scorpions, wild pigs, bears, and vampire bats.

Seriously committed, I finally found a paint of cream-colored stones that would do. Spreading out my sleeping bag, I brushed away ants the size of grasshoppers. Snuggling into the bag, I watched the sunset paint the clouds and the valley below with shades of pink and apricot, then with deep brown, and finally pitch black.

I fell fitfully asleep. Sometime during the night, the full moon having risen high overhead, I awoke suddenly, filled with terror. What was that I heard? Footsteps? A rattler swishing through the brush? I could hear only the beating of my heart and my rapid breaths. I could see nothing with my flashlight. Was this terror merited? What if it was not just my imagination?

I remembered, then, a life-threatening encounter from a decade earlier. Another warm, moonlit night—that time, I had been sleeping in the safety of my own bed. A burglar, looking for drug money, had crawled in through an open window. Grabbing me out of bed, he put a straight-edged razor to my throat and told me to give him all my cash.

Instinctively, I led the burglar to a drawer I rarely opened. In fact, I had no idea what was inside. When I opened it up, I knew immediately that there would be no money to be found in the drawer. But there was a sharp pair of scissors. Before I could think, I grabbed it out, wheeled around, and thrust at him. The surprise of my gutsy action, more than the strength of my stab, shocked him into releasing me, and I fled down several flights of stairs to safety.

As I thought of this incident in the light of the full desert moon, I suddenly understood that my great terror was no less than the manifestation of my great desire to live.

"Who's there?" I shouted into the desert night, peering into the full moon's shadows for a glimpse of my destiny. I knew I could run toward the light of the retreat below, chased by my terror down the mountainside. But I also knew that if I did that, I would always be afraid of everything. I gathered myself together and proclaimed to my deepest self: Whatever it is that comes to me, I will rise to meet it.

The rustling came closer. What was it this time? In the past, I had always been spared. I had made it through car crashes, job losses, earthquakes, legal papers, serious illness. And yet, I had always been given another chance, over and over again. I remembered the words of the philosopher William James. "Believe, and you shall be right, for you shall save yourself; doubt, and you shall be right, for you shall perish."

Stepping out into the moonlight, I faced the fear that has stalked so much of my life. What I saw was the part of me who I could count on to doubt my competence; who thinks I make stupid choices; who doesn't believe I can make it on my own; who squashes the vitality of others; who thinks I am blowing my life; who thinks other people always know more than me; who is reluctant to share her gifts; who spends so much of her life running away from the unknown in terror.

In short, it was all those qualities I most fear about myself that stepped out of the shadows on that moonlit night on the mountain. But, I realized suddenly, I hadn't thought about the snakes, the bats, the clients—or any of the fearful objects that so often fill my consciousness with terror—for many moments. In fact, instead of running across the desert of my consciousness, chased by real or imagined threats, I simply felt sad.

My terrified shadow stepped forward just as the early rays of the morning sun peaked over the mountaintop. And suddenly, I felt an emotion I had not expected to encounter: compassion. I had survived a dark night. And now I could see the woman before me, not only as someone who spent much of her life chased by fear—but as someone who, despite all, *had accomplished as much as she had*. I realized that every time I pitied myself for my inadequacies, I had been denying the truth: my very desire to hope for something more out of life, my terror that expressed the urgency of my will to live, my willingness to stretch beyond the boundaries of comfort. I was competent and courageous, too. In the dawn of that special day, I felt magical words form in my heart.

"You don't need a wake-up call if you are already awake."

From that moment on, the desert lost its terror for me. Upon returning to work, I knew that I had the choice of being a victim of circumstances—or I could choose to be initiated by them. In the following days, as I returned to daily life, with its potential for cruelty, disrespect, abuse, bad luck, failed results, and more, I witnessed my internal process moving to a new stage of growth.

It wasn't long before I had the opportunity to test this new stage out. Soon after returning to work, we made a strategic decision to invest all of our agency's resources to go after a big, new client in the computer industry. Believing that we were the top contender, we depleted our cash reserves putting together a speculative campaign. We neglected the new client leads that came along, using our time to instead master our prospect's specialized industry. The presentation went as planned and we thought for sure that we had won the account. In fact, given our cash flow—we had better have won the business. Instead, a too-thin envelope arrived by messenger, giving us the bad news: Another agency had been selected.

But like the farmer and the horse, this isn't the end of the story. Without wasting any time, we shifted into high gear, resurrecting the neglected leads for possible clients. Before we could make even our first call, the phone rang. An even larger computer industry company in the same area of specialization as the one who'd passed us up was on the line. The marketing director had heard that their competition was sharpening their marketing axe by hiring an agency. Did we know anything about the field?

Did we! All those weeks of prepping. We were raring to go! Had we been hired by the first firm we would not have been free to handle this client, who had a bigger budget than the account we'd been denied.

You can't know the future: what is going to happen to you next. The real test of character is not whether you can keep the faith when things are going your way—but rather, how you do when the ship is breaking up beneath you?

In the Hasidic tradition, rabbis have passed the story of the oil merchant Rachamim from generation to generation.

Rachamim was a wealthy man, living in comfort. When the spiritual master known as the Baal Shem Tov happened upon Rachamim's village during his travels, it was natural for the oil merchant to offer the master his hospitality. At the conclusion of his pleasant stay, the Baal Shem Tov offered to grant Rachamim the blessing of his choice. Rachamim had but one wish: a guaranteed place in the world to come. Hearing this, the Baal Shem Tov sighed, replying at last, "Bring some wagonloads of wine to my home and I will grant your wish."

The oil merchant busied himself with the task. He loaded his wagons and for many days, led his caravan over the countryside. One night, it began to storm. The dirt roads turned to mud and Rachamim was forced to seek shelter. He settled his wagons, horses, and drivers into an empty warehouse, traveling by foot to a nearby inn.

When he awoke the next morning, something was terribly amiss. He found the warehouse—but the wine, horses, wagons, and drivers were gone. He rushed back to the inn to seek help—but the inn had also disappeared. Just then, a group of beggars came upon him.

"Have I lost my way?" he asked. "Where is the inn? Where is the warehouse?"

They replied, "You are mistaken. There's no inn, no warehouse near here."

Rachamim sank to the ground.

"What am I to do?" he cried. Far from family and home, with no transportation or resources, he was lost. The beggars conferred. He could join them, they offered. Rachamim assented, while feeling the full brunt of his sorrow, never once succumbing to bitterness about his loss.

After many months wandering from village to village, the band of beggars arrived at last in the home village of the Baal Shem Tov. Sensing Rachamim's arrival, the master sent for the beggars, preparing for Rachamim the seat of honor.

"Do you remember the last time we met?" the Baal Shem Tov asked him. "You asked me for a place in the world to come. You believed that all you needed was my blessing. But my blessing, alone, could not prepare you for that which you've asked."

The Baal Shem Tov explained that Rachamim had impressed him with his great hospitality. But having a good heart, alone, is not enough to warrant a place in the world to come. If one has a pleasant life, goodness can come easily, the Baal Shem Tov explained. But to have everything taken away and not become bitter, this is how one becomes worthy of such a blessing as Rachamim desired.

At last, his wish was granted. Rachamim eventually returned home, his worldly goods restored. But as happy as he was to have them back, they meant little compared to his greatest attainment: a heart that had shown itself strong and steady regardless of whatever fate sent his way.

When you give up your endless fascination with how inadequate you've been, how often you've been let down, you begin to understand the magnitude of what it means to live life fully. Giving up the illusion of control, you find comfort in the only place of refuge left: compassion for yourself and for the human condition.

When you can do this, you begin to value, above all, those moments of courage, wisdom, and love that demonstrate the nobility we each have, in our earnest efforts to deal with the bittersweet realities of life. The boss who drops unjust anger mid-rage to acknowledge and apologize for her misdirected emotion; the businessman who brushes himself off from failure to try again; the musician who supports himself by being a waiter, who replenishes the coffee before your cup is empty; the stenographer, afraid of conflict, who walks through her terror to take a recalcitrant client to court to collect on services rendered. These are just a few examples.

You think you know what's best for you—what you really want. But what if it truly does not matter what job title you've attained, whether you get the car you think you deserve, whether you live in the right house in the right suburb, or whether your kids attend the most prestigious schools?

What if our society has become confused about external manifestations as if they were the sole measure of your success—when, at best, they are simply by-products of the pursuit of your real purpose? What if the only thing that really matters is that you develop in yourself those deeper spiritual qualities that contribute to the continued evolution of life on our planet? Qualities like character, faith, compassion, and love.

If this were true, you could stop whipping yourself to make your career or business happen. Instead of pushing and protecting, you would find your real destiny deep inside your heart beckoning to you to let it unfold. You keep stuffing your spirit to be responsible. But where is your real responsibility? To do whatever you can to awaken to your innate capacity to respond to your highest spiritual impulses. This is the only path worth walking: the life-long journey that will lead you to fulfill your true human potential.

Do this and you disconnect at last from anxiety over whether you're earning enough points to justify your existence. You can begin to trust that regardless of the circumstances in which you find yourself, you can always have the most supreme experience in the world: the experience of being fully alive.

Affirmation

I have compassion for myself and for the human condition.

Principle Number Five

When you are driven by life, the odds will be with you.

———

*I*f these principles were simply a matter of showing the way to clearing away destructive beliefs, it would be enough. You would have access to previously untapped wellsprings of courage and creativity. People would find themselves attracted to the vitality of your spirit. You would have a better grasp of reality. Out of this, you would be able to manage your worklife more effectively.

But I believe there's much more. When you are courageous enough to challenge your beliefs and take up the task of being fully alive, you create an increased opportunity for forces beyond your comprehension to become engaged in your success.

Does this sound irrational? There are many things that happen to us every day that defy explanation: spontaneous remission of illness; premonition of news; coincidence; intuition; luck.

Think of the downsized worker who, on the brink of financial disaster, prays for deliverance and the phone rings with a job offer. Or how about the lawyer, pressed to meet a trial date, who breaks a tooth requiring an emergency visit to the dentist. Thumbing through old magazines in the reception room, she stumbles across exactly the inspiration for the opening she needs.

Once upon a time, eclipses, rainstorms, gravity, and fire were inexplainable phenomena in terms of existing science. Over millennia, each was incorporated into rational understanding, explained by laws of physics and chemistry. As we are in the beginning stages of a new millennium, who is to say whether those things that you now consider "irrational" won't someday also be explained by some known — or yet to be discovered — law? Do you need to understand how electricity works before flipping on the lights? Of course not. And you would be equally foolish to wait for someone to scientifically prove that there is some mysterious force working on your behalf before you began to trust your intuitive experience.

You need only to observe nature over time to see that actions that promote life have a greater tendency to succeed than those that promote the suppression of life. Begin with your own biology. New life begins with the release of billions of sperms into a hostile environment, driven by mysterious forces, competing amongst themselves, to reach the goal of fertilization. Only one will succeed. The very fact that you have come into existence is miraculous.

The universe can be counted on to support new growth. What is born, over time, has always exceeded that which passes away. Think of the ability of your forebearers to survive the perils of nature and history. Or our perilous current times and the survival of civilization despite access to unprecedented tools of destruction. The continuing existence of life on this planet defies logic.

You carry within you the inheritance of these miracles: a lifeforce that follows a continuous thread of existence back to the very beginning of time. As a link in the chain that finds both its roots and its destiny in the unknown, you are entrusted in this particular time and place with a sacred responsibility. You are no less than the contemporary embodiment of lifeforce: You are not its source, but rather, the most current vehicle of its expression.

Having spent time presenting proposals to various clients over the years, I witnessed in myself and my staff a curious phenomenon. As professionals, we could be counted on to present our material, informing or educating audiences in a competent manner. But every once in awhile, there are those moments when the technique seems to drop away and suddenly we are connecting into a mysterious energy flow. At these rare moments, clients are more than influenced by the presentation. They are moved.

Carl Jung, one of the founding fathers of modern psychology, spent thirty years thinking about such mysterious phenomenon, along with incidents of luck, coincidence, and chance.

Perhaps you have heard the term "synchronicity." According to Jung, synchronicity takes the apparently accidental nature of such phenomenon as meaning "something more" than mere chance. In fact, what Jung named was the interrelationship of everything. Every action, no matter how minor, carries ramifications that interact infinitely — subtly or not — with the whole. On an external level, we can see this when we focus our attention on our ecologically sensitive planet. Use hairspray in New Jersey and the hole in the ozone layer over Antarctica enlarges. Pollute a stream in one time zone and the cows in another produce less milk. In government, too, a global economy has linked us together. When the currency plunges on a small island on the other side of the world, a financial tidal wave sweeps through markets around the globe.

The spiritually inspired thought "we are all one" takes on new meaning as we begin to understand that at any given moment, every action that is taking place on the planet is somehow related to every other past, simultaneous, and future action.

But Jung wasn't only thinking about external actions. His concept of synchronicity penetrated into the recesses of our very hearts and minds. In studying ancient forms of divination, he sought to explain how and why the apparently random chance of tossing sticks, casting coins, or pulling a particular card could result in intelligent, targeted insight beyond what accident alone could produce. He came to believe that because everything is interconnected, the card you seem to pull randomly from a deck is, in truth, part of a larger pattern. It is, in fact, the culmination of all the forces at play in the universe at that particular moment, including your own subconscious thoughts.

What synchronicity does is give a name to what you have most probably intuited to be true in your own experience: There is a connection between your spiritual, emotional, and psychological states and the things that happen to you.

There is an ancient Chinese story that illustrates this point:

A small village was suffering from a devastating drought. A rainmaker was summoned to perform a magical ritual. When he arrived, he said he would not be able to begin for some time. He asked for a hut away from the village and five days' worth of food. On the fourth day, it began to rain. The villagers rushed to his hut to thank him. But the rainmaker protested that he had not yet performed the ceremony.

When he arrived in the village, he explained, he had been feeling anxious and fearful. He had spent the time in the hut calming himself in order to perform the ritual. The moment he became fully relaxed, the rains came. Such was the power of his commitment that the rectification of his internal process swept along the rectification of the climate in its wake.

We are all capable of creating environments in which a connection to the lifeforce is most likely to occur. Actors, professional speakers, musicians, and artists are perhaps more aware than most of us of this connection. I know one speaker who used to be terrified of her audience's power to judge her. An experienced meditator, she knew she could feel connection to the lifeforce when sitting alone with her eyes closed. Why not when standing before a thousand people in a municipal auditorium? She began experimenting, taking a moment before she started to speak to visualize the lifeforce as a white light entering into her through the top of her head, flowing like waves of shimmering light from her mouth over the seated audience. It worked. By doing this simple visualization, she was able to move beyond her fear of judgement and experience the hearts of those who came to hear her speak opening to her. Not only was she more relaxed and confident, but her audiences now routinely give her highest marks.

The more you clear out the stress and effort associated with the destructive beliefs addressed in previous chapters, the more you uncover your innate potential to consciously tap into the lifeforce as you go about your daily activities.

If you program your internal computer with this new belief, you can start swimming with, rather than against, the current by managing your worklife as if your well-being, and the well-being of those who populate your workplace matter. When your actions are consistent with your highest spiritual aspirations, you experience the spontaneous support of the universe. Rather than feel that the more you do, the farther behind you fall, you feel that for every step you take, you move a yard.

I had the good fortune of experiencing this principle in action not long after the agency moved our offices uptown to San Francisco's Union Street. The street of boutiques and restaurants is famous as the place to go for many of the world's most precious gift items. But when we moved our offices there, we soon discovered what was to be the rarest and most sought after of its many offerings: a parking space.

Our lease included one. I should have guessed what lay in store for me when the landlord's fine print included the disclaimer that he would not be responsible for towing trespassers.

To get to this parking space, you must first discover that the crack between two Victorian buildings, which looks as if it might be left over from the Great Quake of '06, is actually an alley leading to a private parking lot. Once you position your vehicle for entry, you ease between the walls, careful to avoid the wooden post at the corner that has been scraped so often you can see the whorls that were growing when Columbus discovered America.

Then, if you are lucky, all you need to do is remove a crate or a couple of bags of decaying vegetable matter overflowing from the garbage dumpster that shares your space to make room for your car. To enter, you wildly crank the steering wheel right and then left, timing the release of the brake and the application of gas in a complex synthesis of discipline and motion.

I soon came to realize that renting a private parking space anywhere in the vicinity of Union Street is somewhat akin to buying a deed to the Brooklyn Bridge.

Every time I pulled down the skinny alley to this troubled parking space, it was occupied. If it wasn't the guy who owned the shop next door, unloading supplies for his window display, it was a friend of one of the apartment dwellers nearby. There were messengers, loan applicants, shoppers, diners, drinkers, and women with ragged nails desperate to make their appointments with their manicurists.

How they even found the space was astonishing, but that they braved our increasingly threatening collection of signs—"You Will Be Towed" and "Do Not Even Think of Parking Here"—was perversely impressive.

I learned to herald my arrival with angry honks. Often the guilty party could be summoned thusly, attuned to the abrasive sound like dog to whistle. Fueled by righteous anger, my blood and tongue would race. With fist shaking, I'd watch as they'd angle back and forth, frantic for escape, finally clearing the way and racing to freedom.

Whatever triumph I felt through this primitive exchange was usually offset by the residue of anger that, once released, refused to depart. They rode off to steal somebody else's space, and I was left with a churning stomach.

Then there was the day, car poised for entry, when I was unwilling to go through this drama one more time. Preparing to beat my chest, I instead found myself taking a small but decisive step on behalf of the evolution of the planet. As I thought of the press of humanity, questing for nothing more than my chunk of concrete under the sun, I stopped fighting and instead made an internal offering.

Anger hadn't worked. What if I blessed them? Wished to those less fortunate than I that they get exactly what they want in their lives. Surely, I did not want the messenger to be unable to deliver his packages.

Yes, I do want them to get what they want. But, of course, I preferred if they could get it some other way than inconveniencing me. If that was not possible, however, I would give them my space as a gift. There would be other battles more worth fighting, I knew. Pass on this, and I would have my full energy available to me when I might truly need it. I would from this point on pick my battles more carefully.

There have, indeed, been other battles. But seldom have they been about where to park my car. Because after that day, the space had seldom been unlawfully occupied. Each time I rounded the corner into the crack, I recreated once more the willingness to share my space, and more often than not, I found the open space welcoming me.

Through trial and error, I have discovered that when I call upon my highest spiritual aspirations (generosity, faith, compassion, and the like) rather than my lowest (greed, self-righteousness, laziness, and so on) I tip the scales in the direction of the most favorable outcome possible. As I said earlier in chapter three, many influences will contribute to the resolution of our issues, and your hope becomes one of those factors. Perhaps it is but a very small consideration, but even so, your highest aspirations may carry just enough weight to make the difference.

When we left off our discussion about affirmations on p. 93, I maintained that it was preferable for you to sit in pain and irresolution than to seek superficial or premature resolution. So what if you are one of those people whose jagged-edged beliefs are still cycling around in your brain in an endless loop?

I'm sunk. This time, I've really gotten in over my head. I'm sick and tired of feeling this bad. I'm so alone. The world is against me. I've got nowhere to turn. I'm so ashamed.

Because the words seem so justified, you hang on to them. But there can come a time when authentic pain rising to consciousness crosses the line and becomes a bad habit. If left to your own devices, it is possible to become enthralled with your unhappiness. At times like these, consider the possibility that your grievances could have someplace to go where they could get things moving again.

Where is this place? Send them to the heart of the universe, where anything is possible. This is what the author of Psalm 69:1-5 did. In fact, the complaints we are working with in this exercise are nothing more than a contemporary interpretation of that Biblical passage.

Here's how to do it. This time, as you witness the droning words of complaint looping through your mind, simply insert your name for the divine periodically. For practice, go ahead and fill in these blanks.

_____, *I'm sunk. This time, I've really gotten in over my head. I'm sick and tired of feeling so bad.* _____, *I'm so alone. The world is against me. I've got nowhere to turn.* _____, *I'm so ashamed.*

By addressing your grievances to a power greater than yourself, you make your complaints potent. Tempered by hope, your complaints can now enliven rather than deplete you.

I have applied this discovery to everything from filing taxes to developing business strategies. During a period of recession, our agency's new business efforts skidded to a halt. Despite our massive outreach to new clients, the business climate in San Francisco was basically on hold for two months. Our associate Harvey, bemoaning the problems that had beset his advertising firm, commented that he understood the reluctance of potential clients to sign on the dotted line.

"I'm so insecure about the future of the world, I'm afraid to make any commitment longer-term than ordering a piece of pie," Harvey admitted.

Hitting the phones every day, Dan and I realized that fear was driving us down the fast track to burnout. Rather than continue to push upstream, we decided to take a different approach. We would follow up responsibly with those prospects who had indicated interest. But beyond that, we would take our vital energy and invest it in whatever channels remained open to us. Dan took the time to get more involved with the Public Relations Society of America, a national professional organization, taking a leadership role that he knew would position him as an industry expert in a developing areas of new business. The time he put into the position would be of little use to us now, but he had faith that someday the winds would shift—and we would be ready. We also spent more time with our family, nurturing our little unit. We took special care of our spirits, taking time to meditate and to record our thoughts in journals. If you had asked us what we were doing about new business during this period, we would have answered honestly, "We prayed a lot."

The day the stock market reversed its downward trend, the phones starting ringing. We believed that fate would complete its cycle of misfortune. Sooner or later, it always does. And it did. By using the time of uncertainty to revitalize and nurture ourselves and those around us, we emerged from the crisis with our spirits intact. There was a pent-up demand for our services and we were ready, able, and willing to rise to the occasion and get out of the red. In fact, the industry Dan targeted proved to be a wise choice. Business boomed beyond the expectations of our interrupted trajectory.

On the other hand, some of our associates who had relied on the strength of their wills to push against the times in order to stay in the black, greeted that same day with exhaustion and resentment. In the months that followed, San Francisco experienced a frenzy of mergers and acquisitions as little companies, spirits broken by the recession, sold out for bargain basement prices.

When I gave an early version of this manuscript to one of my clients, he simply could not buy the thought that if you are driven by life rather than fear, the odds will be with you. A hard-driving executive in the insurance business, Sam fervently believed that he had achieved his lofty success through the strength of his will and hard work.

"I've struggled for everything—and it hasn't been easy," he explained to me in the back seat of his limousine as we returned from an interview with a business page reporter. Accompanying us on our ride that day were his raging ulcer and a pronounced nervous tic.

Sam pulled out what he considered to be the secret of his success. It was a carefully-crafted chart, in which every twenty-four-hour day of the week was divided into fifteen-minute segments. Using brightly colored felt tip pens, he had designated red blocks for meetings with his subordinates. Massive amounts of purple signified meetings with potential clients. There were huge swatches of yellow, black, and orange.

"What's that little bit of green?" I asked, pointing to a slender stripe across the bottom of the page.

"That's time for family, fun, and relaxation."

As we turned the corner to my office, I asked him why he had such a problem with the concept of inner excellence.

"It's not that I don't see where you're coming from," he replied. "It's just that while it may be true that the universe wants *you* to succeed, it sure as heck doesn't want me to. Everything I've accomplished, I've had to do on my own."

In that moment, I had an inspiration.

"What if," I boldly ventured "it wasn't your willpower that got you your results? What if your results came *despite* your willpower? What if you let up, spent some time nurturing yourself and your family, contributing to the community—and experienced even greater success?"

"You may be right," he said finally. "But I am not willing to take the risk of finding out that I am the exception to your rule." Popping Maalox, Sam rode off into his next swatch of red.

Sam is far from alone. Receiving an invitation to address several hundred men and women at a chamber of commerce function in a town known for its dedication to hard work, I wondered how I could ever convince a roomful of potential Sams to at least consider the possibility that there could be a positive connection between spirituality and success. When I discussed this with Dan, he proposed that I point out that each one of them undoubtedly had on their person, that very day, a symbol of this radical new concept.

"You must be kidding," I replied.

Then Dan reached into his pocket and pulled out a well-worn dollar bill.

"*Annuit Coeptis*," he read aloud. "Latin for 'He looks with favor upon our undertaking.'"

Did our forefathers share my belief that a force greater than ourselves really does want us to succeed?

Research led me to the late historian and visionary Dr. Willis Harman's book, *Global Mind Change* (Warner). Harman points out that the design of the dollar bill was set in 1782. The symbolism was inspired by the transcendental spirituality of Freemasonry. In fact, fifty of the fifty-six signers of the Declaration of Independence, including Benjamin Franklin and George Washington, were Masons. The roots of our economic systems hail back to these potent images, clearly drawing the connection between spiritual principles and economic success.

The Great Seal of the United States of America, for example, features an unfinished pyramid topped by the omnipotent eye of the divine. This symbol communicates to us that while we can accomplish much on our own, our work is incomplete unless inspired by a power greater than ourselves.

Synchronicity—the interrelationship between our inner and outer worlds—is a challenging concept for many of us. If you are still resistant to the concept, you will have to ask yourself a fundamental question: Do you think that this is a universe in which order is the norm and chaos the exception? Or do you believe that this is a basically chaotic universe with order belong an occasional accidental coincidence? Inner excellence is predicated on the assumption that there is an unseen order to the universe supportive of your spiritual evolution and expanding experience of success, even if it often feels to us as if chaos lurks beneath our own efforts to control and protect. Of course you have your own agenda, particularly when it comes to your livelihood. You think you know what job would be best for you, how much you should be earning, how the relationships should be in your workplace. But destiny does not always seem to pay heed to your preferences and timetables.

You can't "make" the connection to divine order happen. All you can do, like the rainmaker in his hut, is create the environment in which connection to the lifeforce is most likely to take place. Divine order is mysterious, beyond our understanding and control.

And then, too, there are those moments when you are graced with the in-breaking of the divine for no apparent reason. Without doing anything in particular, you find yourself tapped into the sense that everything somehow makes sense—and that it is good. When you are in alignment with the unseen order, you have what Jews call *mazel*—luck. In the Hasidic tradition, mazel is translated to mean an influencing configuration of higher forces.

But don't settle the questions about order versus chaos too quickly. In fact, Albert Einstein once suggested that the only question every human being must ask him or herself is whether this universe is friendly or not? Given that there are so often discrepancies between what we think we want and what the universe seems to deliver to us, just exactly what does it mean to say that there is an unseen order supportive of your success? In this day of arbitrary injustice—drive-by shootings and hostile takeovers, not to mention genocide and holocaust—the traditional concept of a God who rewards and punishes our behavior with material success has become rightfully eroded. God is not our cosmic delivery boy, nor are we God's puppets. But there are new understandings of God pointed towards in the forward-thinking aspects of many of the world's religious traditions—from constructive Christianity and the Jewish renewal movement, process theology and deep ecology to feminist thought in dialogue with Eastern traditions—that hold the promise of a vital relationship to the divine that can withstand any test.

In this new understanding, God is active in our lives as a present moment that is always free and full of possibilities. God is the mysterious summons that persuades us towards the greatest good possible. We have the freedom of will to choose to do those things in keeping with our highest aspirations—or our lowest. By heeding the impulse to choose good, we contribute to the creation of a better future than would otherwise have occurred. Some days you get exactly what you would have hoped for. Some days you do not. What you can always trust is this: The best possible outcome under the circumstances is always available to us. Even under the most challenging circumstances, it is always possible to experience connection to the divine.

Beneath the pyramid on the American dollar bill are the words of Virgil: *"Novus Ordo Seclorum"* or "A new order of the ages is born." As I strode onstage that night, a dollar bill firmly clenched in hand, my ideas no longer seemed so radical. Our entire economic system is based on images that bear a striking resemblance to the same thoughts that Sam the insurance executive found so incredulous. Is this "new order" none other than the spirituality and business movement that today's organizational consultants are bringing to forward-thinking corporations around the world?

What if you made your decisions based on your faith that you are not judged on the results of your life to date? The sacrifices you have failed to make? The goals you have not yet achieved? What if the universe does not need evidence from you that your existence is justified? What if every moment were fresh and new for you to choose life and love over fear-driven behaviors and selfish concerns? Correcting old mistakes, contributing to the greater good, making your work and life a blessing?

Would it really matter whether or not you could replicate inner excellence in a scientific laboratory? Maybe I can't prove to you that the universe is urging you towards the best possible outcome—but can you prove to me that it's not? Not even the greatest scientist of our time can know something as basic as when time began; or where the outer boundaries of the cosmos may be found. How can you be so sure of your beliefs?

What I longed to explain to Sam is that the miracles I had been experiencing in the transformation of my own career and business did not come just from my loving life—but from life loving me. I approach every day believing that when I make the choices that are in keeping with my highest aspirations, whatever happens to me is evidence of God's support of my growth and development as a human being. It is with the development of my character and spirit, not my results, that my loyalty lies.

You can become so enthralled with this process, you may well forget what it was you thought you wanted in the first place. If you are among the few who are courageous enough to acquire an appreciation for life's complexities, you will never run out of fascinating material. The ultimate gift is not that you will get what you think you want, but that you can come to genuinely appreciate what you get.

Affirmation

By responding to the entreaties of my heart, I contribute to the creation of a better future than would otherwise have occurred.

Principle Number Six

Your ordinary self is enough.

———✦———

Eastern mystics tell the story of the disciples of two masters who live across the river from one another. One day, the disciples happen upon each other. The first shouts across the river bank.

"My teacher can manifest jewels in the palms of his bare hands. He can stand on this bank of the river and paint a canvas on the other side with the image of his choice. He can levitate and he can change himself into a tiger. What miraculous things can your teacher do?"

"Only this," said the second. "When he's hungry, he eats. When he's tired, he sleeps."

When you are living life fully, you are not doing things you think of as great. You merely do what's next. You are not pushed at a self-destructive pace by fear. Turning a deaf ear to the sirens of false promise, you no longer work so intensely that you sacrifice your long-term well-being. You set your pace by monitoring your vitality. You know you are pushing too hard if you start to burn out; if you get bored, you aren't stretching enough.

There are many times when you are confused about what is next for you to do. Should you leave your safe, stale job to take the risk of changing positions? Should you live off your life savings for a year to get an advanced degree? Should you pass up the promotion because you want to protect the time you have to spend with your family? Should you do this or do that?

Perhaps you have not considered the possibility that what is next for you is to sit in confusion for awhile. When you are clear about what is next, answer the call. When you aren't, pause.

Sometimes you will be inspired, sometimes you will feel lost. You will make mistakes along the way and you will learn from your mistakes. Even this you won't do perfectly.

Over the years, I have monitored the progress of a friend of mine, one of the Bay Area's premiere bakers. When I first met Elliot, he was working in a jewelry factory—a dead-end job that was burning him out and wasting his talents. What Elliot loved to do was bake. I first sampled Elliot's passion—a rich cheesecake based on his family's recipe—at a potluck party. I'm sure I was one of the many people who said to him, "You really should do something with this."

Eventually, Elliot was able to raise seed money to open a little bakery. Sometimes as a friend and patron— sometimes as his bakery's public relations agent— I watched Elliot progress as I munched more samples of various new flavors of cheesecake than I care to confess.

Of course Elliot wanted to make money. But it was critical to him how and why he went about achieving his goals. First of all, it was important to him that this cheesecake—and any other bakery goods he added to his line of offerings—stay true to his family's high standards. Secondly, he wanted his growing staff to be more than coworkers. He hoped that they would develop into a true community.

The response was phenomenal, and soon Elliot's one little bakery grew into a regional chain of bakeries, not only selling retail to happy customers but to restaurants and gourmet shops throughout California. As the chain grew, management problems crept in. He sought out consultants who guided him to experiment with various management styles and formats. New cakes made bold debuts then quietly slipped away into oblivion. Some bakery locations worked. Some didn't. The corporation's numbers slipped, slid, and soared depending on the season, the personnel, and a thousand other factors. But through it all, Elliot stayed true to his original vision. Above all, he wanted to share his family's cheesecake with others. His chain of bakeries and wholesale operation are now a multimillion dollar empire, as well known for its generous contributions to the community and for its proud employees as it is for its delicious cheesecake.

Elliot trusted that his greatest success would come not despite the nurturing of his highest aspirations—but because of it.

Here's another example of someone for whom spirit and character come first—one you may never read about in *Fortune* or *Forbes*. On a media tour promoting my book, I was met at the airport by Delores, one of the producers of a national cable television program, operating outside of Washington, D.C. I was struck by her serenity. My awe increased as she told me that she had just recently discovered that the funding for the program had fallen short and that she was on the final day of her job with no new opportunity yet in sight.

"When I came here several years ago, I wanted to break into broadcasting more than anything in the world.

I loaded all my belongings into my VW and pulled into town. I put in my application and called every day. I was down to my last dollar, but I trusted that something would happen for me."

Indeed, Delores got the job offer within days.

Now, several years later, Delores was dropping me off at the studio—her last task before going home to pack her bags.

"How can you be so composed at a time like this?" I asked.

"Simple. When I first heard about problems here, I started praying. I let God know that my preference—given my limited perspective—was to stay in this job. But I also asked that if this were not what I am meant to do any more, that this door be closed."

Delores explained to me that in her life, every time a door closed, sooner or later, another door opened. Sometimes, even by her own admission, the timing of doors slamming shut and others swinging open was less than ideal. She felt that it was in those difficult transitional periods that she did the most growing.

Even as I listened, I tempered my awe of Delores with the quiet suspicion that her faith may have been derived from an insufficient data base. As the older, more experienced woman I imagined myself to be at the time, I came away wondering if the key to her serenity was that she was young and privileged enough to not have experienced real pain yet. While I aspired to the sweet simplicity of her faith, I have personally not been able to solve the riddle of how to be more fully conscious without also being more fully afraid.

In fact, following the principles of inner excellence, I have more readily come face to face with feelings and emotions that I was once able to avoid through external diversion. Haven't you noticed how many highly ambitious people become uncomfortable when things get too quiet around them? How many fast-track people do you know who routinely avoid laid-back vacations, such as sitting with a good book on a peaceful beach, in favor of attending a competitive tennis camp or hitting ten European cities in twelve days? The other day, I was cherishing a quiet moment walking the unpaved paths around my favorite city park, Radnor Lake when I passed by an executive putting in her hour's exercise in nature while making deals on her cell phone!

Many people say they don't have an inner voice of wisdom, or that they don't know which voice is the "real" one. The truth is that many of us know exactly what would be right or best for us to do. We simply don't want to admit it because we are so afraid of what our inner voice will tell us to do. What if your inner voice is telling you to do something to shake up the comfort of the status quo? Take a risk to serve a higher purpose in your life? Rectify a wrong? Or what if your inner voice is telling you that you can't have what you think you want? Or that you don't really want what you have worked so hard to achieve?

Edward Allen Toppel is an independent floor trader who spent nearly twenty years in the futures pit in the Chicago Mercantile Exchange, observing people's reluctance to pay attention to their inner voices. On the very day Toppel made some of his greatest profits trading IBM options, he had an enlightening experience, shared in his book *Zen in the Markets: Confessions of a Samurai Trader*.

The crux of what he discovered is this: There are only four rules of trading and investing if you want to make money on the stock exchange. "1. Buy low, sell high. 2. Let profits run, cut losses quickly. 3. Add to a winning position, not a loser. 4. Go with the trend."

Sounds easy. So why do so many people play the stock market and end up losing? Toppel explains that people ignore their inner voice that knows these rules. When things start to slip, "Ego starts to tighten its grip over our ability to do the right thing. The right thing is to get rid of the losers immediately. The ego will produce the most fantastic reasons for holding on to that money-draining position, be it in stocks, bonds, options, or futures. Ego will fight us all the way and prevent us from realizing quickly that it is better to swallow our pride and do the right thing."

We think we are clever at avoiding our internal moment of reckoning, but the truth is, if we don't allow our inner voices to rise to consciousness they will make themselves known to us in the form of problems. Even if it's painful to tune into what your heart is telling you, wouldn't you rather know what you are dealing with in your life earlier on, when you will be more likely to do something about it, than to be overtaken again and again by "bad luck" and unwelcome surprises?

This does not, however, mean that when you practice inner excellence, you find the way to eradicate fear. Who among us, awakened from the once comforting illusions that no longer suffice, would not feel trepidation? I have learned that we cannot always count on the serenity of faith to save us from our fears. Perhaps the best we can hope for is to be able to name our terror and be willing to rise to the occasion. The real challenge, in fact, may be not to avoid fear, but rather to extend acceptance to ourselves when we are afraid.

Accessible to me, exposed in the bright light of day, my fears are more apparent to me now than ever before. *But they drive me less.*

If you can find self-acceptance no matter how afraid you are and if things will go wrong no matter how good you are, ask yourself: What's the hurry? Why suffer relentless pressure to achieve and accomplish if you cannot judge your success or failure solely by your results?

Legend has it that Alexander the Great once came upon a saint, sunning himself on the bank of a river.

"Old man, you look so content. What I would give to be able to sit there like you and enjoy the sun!" said Alexander.

The saint laughed, asking Alexander where he was headed.

"I have one last battle to fight. Then I will come back and join you!" he replied.

"You foolish man," said the saint. "Why go to conquer yet another land when all you want to do in the end is sit here in the sun and rest? I've conquered no one. Send your armies home and sit beside me now and enjoy the day."

Alexander spurned the invitation, marching off to what turned out to be his final encounter. He died on the battlefield.

I do not live my entire life basking in the sun on a river bank. But there are moments. You may recall the story about the half-eaten coffee cake on our conference room table, the now sacred object that has come to symbolize the initiation of my journey to inner excellence. Let me tell you now what happened next.

When we stopped reeling from the shock of our employees organizing against us and took the time to think through how we wanted our worklives to be, we called the staff together and announced our intentions to create a more supportive workplace. Perhaps you would have thought that our employees would have celebrated with us. But having been chosen in the first place in part for their scrappiness, many of the twenty-three had thought we'd gone soft. While we talked about providing an environment that would nurture their highest aspirations, their raised eyebrows informed us that many believed that our developing philosophy would merely make us easy to take advantage of. Sure that we were destined to fail, many began filing into our office to report that they had "out of the blue" received this or that job offer. Over a six month period, we went from twenty-three employees and fifteen clients to four employees and three clients.

There are some people who shift to a higher center and life responds with gracious support without pause. We should always hold the possibility that this is how it can be for us. However, it is as or more likely to be true, as it was in our case, that there will be a lag-time between the setting of our new vision and the harvesting of results.

This was how it was for us. It was as if all the straws of our livelihood had been thrown up in the air at once. We had no idea where or how the straws would land. We had no choice but to release our grip on the way things had been. Red ink whispered and then screamed at us as we began to use lines of credit to fund what we believed to be—against all external evidence—a transition, not a demise. As bleak as things appeared, we continued to invest our vital energy in our new beliefs, trusting that if we continued to pay heed to the behests of our highest selves, eventually all the things that appeared to be falling apart would prove themselves, in time, to have been falling together.

Finally, the last of our disgruntled employees left the business. We had already sold our "dream home," but the mortgage on the modest cottage we planned to move to next had not yet come through. The business was losing money and the *New York Times* had not yet dubbed me the queen of simple living. Moving our young son and infant daughter into an inexpensive bed and breakfast and putting most of our possessions into storage, we surrendered virtually all of our trappings.

In a journal entry, I wrote:

> I've marched myself to the edge of my experience, living much of my life in tears. Even so, when I feel the boundaries expand, I am ecstatic. More and more, I realize that I matter. Never again do I have to let the business consume me. I trust that if I continue to pay attention to nurturing my character and spirit, the business will rebuild into something even more expressive of who I really am. Eventually, our living situation will straighten out. I mourn what is passing—but I choose to invest my vital energy in what I really want.
>
> And what is that?
>
> To more and more experience how sweetness for no reason at all feels. Walking towards the kitchen to wash the dishes, suddenly overwhelmed with gratitude and love. This is as good as it gets.

When you allow your disappointments to loosen your grip on the illusion of control, you leave behind externally-determined definitions of success and failure. Out of depths you had not previously known wells up fresh courage. But even as you feel yourself being pulled toward renewed life, beware! The cost is great. There will be times when you will feel as if you have been directed to march off the edge of a cliff, with only the endless void of the infinity below you. Will you ever again find yourself safe on solid ground? If you are always sure that everything will turn out just the way you hope, then you are still clinging to the edge. To be fully alive is to rise and fall on the ever-changing tides of dread and awe. Only when you become willing to embrace the whole range of human experience do you remove the impediments that separate you from a deep connection to the meaning you seek.

The mystic traditions of both western and eastern religions aspire to describe this state. Christian mystic philosopher Charles Kingsley writes: "When I walk the fields, I am oppressed now and then with an innate feeling that everything I see has a meaning, if I could but understand it. And this feeling of being surrounded with truths which I cannot grasp amounts to indescribable awe . . . ." In the Jewish tradition, Rabbi Abraham Joshua Heschel explains, "God is not always silent, and man is not always blind. There are moments in which . . . heaven and earth kiss each other."

In these moments, you have a sense that you are part of a whole, far greater than whatever private disappointments you have suffered. The ability to embrace a broader range of life experiences inspired by the urge for connection with the divine is not a means to an end, but the end itself.

Once you have tasted such an awareness, even if but for a moment, you can begin to trust that there is meaning in your existence that transcends the ups and downs of your life. By living your ordinary life with the courage of awareness, it becomes more and more possible to set aside your primary concerns for safety and comfort in order to pay greater attention to the urge greater than but including yourself that lures you towards the fulfillment of your higher purpose. The truth is that you do not always know where you are heading, but you can begin to be content to be in free fall within the heart of the divine.

Such moments of unity can happen to you regardless of the circumstances of your life at any given time. Even if you do not live permanently in such a state, once you have experienced the in-breaking of the divine, your life begins to pivot around this new, higher center. It's not that you give up your everyday life, envisioning goals, carrying out plans, celebrating or mourning your results, but the drama of your circumstances is now played out against an infinite backdrop of all-encompassing love and mystery.

The Sufis tell this story:

> On his journey to enlightenment, a student came across a spiritual master on the road outside the village.
>
> "Teacher, I am doing everything I can think of. I pray. I meditate. I live in peace and try to do what is right and good. What else can I do?"
>
> The old teacher stood up and held his hands toward heaven. His fingers became like lamps of fire and he said:
>
> "If you will, you can become all flame."

While it is natural to feel anxiety and sadness when you say goodbye to the old, comfortable ways that have brought you to where you are now, you must discipline yourself to also recognize the excitement inherent in the new ways that are birthing. The challenge is in being able to hold everything at the same time, including the pain of having to make tough choices, leaving aspects that have been important in the past behind.

You can forgive yourself for the mistakes you've made—for turning against yourself. Did you lose the perspective of what your work and life are really about? Of course you have insecurities about your motivation, your ability, your sincerity. These doubts are the universe's forge, strengthening the mettle of your character with courage. Become willing to confront the truth about your whole self, the strengths as well as weaknesses. Not as one who proclaims, "Here is my authentic self: You have to love it."

No, you must learn to say simply, "Here I am, flaws and all. While I would prefer your respect, I am willing to take the consequences."

You know you have progressed in your journey to inner excellence when you recognize that you would rather have the pain of consciousness than forfeit authentic experience. Ironically, only when the passion of your spirit takes precedence over what others might think, do you have a self who is fully available to give and receive love.

How many of you are, like Alexander the Great, putting off your moment in the sun until you get one more accomplishment under your belt? When you get your raise, when you land that next client or job, when your kids are in the right college? When you empty your in-basket, you're high. When it fills up again, you're low. But can you, instead, let your life happen all of the time? Full or empty? Success or failure? How about right now? What I have learned is that it is a waste of time to wait for the circumstances of my life to bring me the experience of success I yearn for. It is with the growth of my character and spirit, and not with my results at work, that my loyalty lies.

When you adopt this perspective, what is happening to you at any particular moment loses so much of its inflated significance. You are able to see the bigger picture. You are more effective. People naturally become attracted to you and want more of what you have. Ironically, over the long haul, your greatest external success comes as a by-product of your devotion to inner excellence.

Arriving at the office one Monday morning, I discovered a flurry of press releases, soiled coffee cups, and scratch paper strewn wildly about. Something had happened between the time I'd left early Friday to give a speech out of town and my arrival back at work three days later. In fact, a case settlement had come in for one of our law clients, representing a major food company.

The team assigned to the account had dropped everything to get a release out in a timely manner. Enthused by the challenge, they had risen to the occasion gloriously. Placements were running in legal and general news media publications even as they caught me up on everything that Monday morning.

As is the informal policy of the agency, I suggested that they take comp time to allow themselves to recover and revitalize after their extraordinary effort. Surely other, less stressed staff members could take up the slack. But running on the adrenaline of success, they turned down the offer.

Toward the end of the week, I saw Terry, the senior account executive, sitting at her computer, holding her head. She had a migraine headache.

"Why don't you go home and take a rest?" I suggested.

"Because I'm already falling behind. If I leave now, I'll lose even more ground. In fact, I've rallied the team and we're planning to come in again this weekend."

Drawing on the wisdom of twenty years of business, I knew that this team's health and vitality were worth far more to me and their client than whatever they felt they could accomplish by working every weekend. Great executives get sick, go on vacation, get called on jury duty, and the business survives. The business could survive a weekend off, too.

Terry pulled her "to do" list up on the computer, proof in black and gray that she had read the crisis correctly. But before I would mark it off for her, I asked a favor. Pressing a couple of dollars into her palm, I asked her to go for a long walk and take time to sip an even longer cup of tea. If upon her return she still felt she needed to work non-stop through another weekend, of course she could.

Terry not only walked to the cafe, she walked all the way to the bay. Watching the waves roll in and roll out for an hour or so, she later reported to me that the city seemed so small and far away. As her headache subsided, she began to see that she had geared herself and her team up to a fever pitch. She was on a battle high, exploiting her ability to dominate and control.

Upon her return, she looked at the blinking computer with fresh eyes. As it turned out, many items on the list could wait until next week. The few that needed immediate attention were less time-consuming than she'd feared, and of those few, some could be delegated to other staff members who had the time to take them up again on Monday. She and her team were out by 5 p.m. for a well-earned, long, and guilt-free weekend.

The simpler the life, the easier it is for us to avoid distractions from what it is we really want. The effort to control destiny no longer compels us to action. When we are stressed, anxious, confused, we have the option of ceasing to push against our limitations and wait.

To all those who aspire to bring inner excellence to their work, I dedicate this prayer.

124

Invocation for Inner Excellence

Help me to give up pushing, demanding, and desiring
   specific rewards from my work.
I trust that when I pay attention to the deepest behests of
   my heart,
I am being led to the fulfillment of my greater purpose
   the fastest way possible.

If it seems long and difficult at times, it is because I am a
   beginner.
If I am disappointed or frustrated along the way,
   I simply make whatever corrections I can.
If I can't find anything to correct, I have the patience to
   wait.

When I am tempted to take a short-cut
   that I know does not come from my heart,
Grant me the clarity to see that imitation will merely give
   the illusion of success.
When I compare myself to others,
   help me to turn jealousy into a blessing for them,
   feeling grateful for what I, too, have achieved.
Help me to love myself,
   trusting that when I pay attention to these things —
   given where I've come from and the circumstances
   I face —
I am always doing my best.

When you no longer feel the need to be extraordinary, you can stop driving yourself to damaging extremes.
When you do this, you begin to manage your relationships
and challenges with a lighter but more effective touch. In
place of the pressure to achieve more, you can find it in

your repertoire to simply do nothing, acting again only when you trust yourself to set a pace that is chosen out of inspiration rather than fear. This is the discipline recovering achievers truly need: to cut yourself and the people around you some slack.

Going through a particularly rough January at the agency, I got together with Gerry, a successful and wise friend who makes her living in the high-pressure retail clothing business. I shared with her that every January since I could remember, I dreaded the feeling that I was having to pay for my time off during the holidays by "getting serious" in the new year. I was pushing myself to function as best I could under the circumstances, day after day. But the effort to perform was getting more and more unbearable.

Gerry had an alarmingly simple solution.

"The next time you approach the office, ask yourself how you are feeling. If you feel fine, proceed. If you are freaking out, don't go in."

She told me that she had once stood on the curb across the street from her boutique for more than an hour, overwhelmed by the challenges she faced, not knowing where to begin. As Gerry stood, she gave herself permission to feel upset without the added judgment that it meant anything about her ability to do the job.

While she was giving herself permission to have feelings, she found herself wondering whether an important call she'd been waiting for had come in yet. She daydreamed about a certain sleeve that she felt the urge to sketch. Then suddenly Gerry saw one of her best customers hurrying down the street and rattling the locked door.

"The thing is, I took one look at my customer and realized how terrible she looked. She really needed my help!"

Gerry ran across the street to work.

When you stop pushing, "doing nothing" turns out not to be lost time. Its value is not only recuperative — although that would be benefit enough. When you stop trying to make things happen, controlling and manipulating external reality, you make room to receive breakthrough ideas beyond what your conscious, rational processes could have produced. The mystics have a name for this state. They call it inspiration.

The Greek mathematician Archimedes had such an experience when, having exhausted his left-brain mental capacities working out the principle of specific gravity, he gave himself a break by taking a bath. As he stepped into the tub, he noticed that the water level rose. This experiential clue provided the breakthrough solution he had been seeking. As the story goes, he shot out of the bath and ran stark naked down the streets of ancient Greece shouting, "Eureka!"

Carl Jung, confused and upset about his break with his mentor Sigmund Freud, retreated to his family home to lick his wounds. While there, he found himself on the floor playing children's games. Soon he took his childhood fantasies out into the backyard, building out of stone the villages, towns, and forts he'd imagined as a young boy. Spontaneously, he was overtaken by the realizations that form the basis of Jungian psychology.

To "do nothing" takes far more courage and commitment than many are willing to invest. You don't believe me? Try this on for size. Let's say you have had a problem thrust upon you. You don't know which course of action to take. Clouding things further, you have other responsibilities and deadlines. Your boss is making unrelated demands. Your children or pets are clamoring for attention. Your significant other is feeling neglected. You've got a choice. You can work like a crazy person from sunrise into the wee hours of the night trying to get everything handled once and for all. Or you could take an hour or two away from the frenzy, shut the door, turn off the phone, and trust that the breakthrough you are yearning for will come more readily to a relaxed and open mind than to a cramped and desperate one.

Do you see what I mean? Of course it takes courage to stop beating down your potential for big, juicy break-throughs with avalanches of reactive little thoughts and actions. Take the time to ponder, to appreciate, to day-dream. When you have faith, you can choose when and how to make room for your intuitive spirit to have its moment. You surrender the arrogance of your controlled intellect to bask patiently in the world of obscured images, plans, and knowledge pressing, as if of their own accord, to take shape.

Even the Japanese, whose proclivity for long hours at work resulted in the modern tragedy of karoshi, honor the value of daydreaming in the midst of their workday. In most American offices, if a worker is seen to be staring blankly out the window, the boss is apt to assume the worker is either slacking off or hasn't been given enough to do. In Japan, however, the daydreamer is left alone. The quiet time is treated with honor and respect.

In their autobiographies, western tycoons and politi cians often brag about the intensity with which they work. Not only do they set a breakneck pace throughout the day, but many report cutting back their hours of sleep to as few as possible. As effective as these high-achievers may be, they are cheating themselves and the world of their freest, wildest, and potentially most productive cre-ativity: access to the unconscious that does not even occur when they are awake. Sleeping is not wasted time. Your brain processes the day's information and reorganizes itself into higher states of knowing than you are capable of achieving through rational processes alone. Your dreams overflow with visual puns, clever juxtapositions, and heroic symbolism that provide precious keys to your inner universe. But scientists have discovered that this can happen only in the deep state of rest that occurs at the end of a full night of uninterrupted sleep. Who knows how even more effective and inspired you might be if you got yourself a good night's sleep?

When I surveyed people from a wide range of occupations and positions, my correspondents reported a variety of useful intuitive practices. A publishing company in Alabama set aside an office for employees to take an afternoon nap. The CEO of a computer company takes a long walk before making important decisions. The presidents of several record companies in Nashville invested in a center for meditation, chanting, and massage within easy walking distance from their offices. When a salesman in Portland, Oregon, realizes that he is becoming overinvested in his results, he puts the phone down and does crossword puzzles.

Some companies, like Apple Computers, offer paid sabbaticals. In fact, fundamental to the Apple legacy is the story about former CEO John Sculley who shocked the computer industry by taking his time-out not long after taking the reins of the company.

He took off for his ranch in Maine where he designed a barn and took a photography class. He returned with plans to streamline management, doing away with many of the company's routine meetings. Upon his return, he quadrupled Apple's revenues to more than $4 billion.

And in case you were wondering, it isn't only high-tech companies and the entertainment industry that are showing the way. *Utne Reader* reports that every Friday, half a dozen federal employees gather for meditation and other spiritual rituals in a quiet conference room. Where? The Pentagon.

Cultivating entry into the world of inner excellence is a patient process, requiring utmost gentleness. Your greatest inspirations and insights are like the most tender sprouts: They simply cannot push up through the concrete of the busy edifices that comprise your daily routine.

You must learn to tend your inner garden, not only in the harvest of the fall, but through the long, empty winter, when you are called upon to invest faith in meditations, in contemplation, in dreams that do not seem to make any sense, in unformed feelings that make you restless, in yearnings that have no object and no names. When you let go of your reliance on the rational, you discover that your efforts to control reality had, in truth, limited your options.

Give up the need to keep control and let yourself be surprised.

Affirmation

I nurture myself at a pace supportive of my overall vitality.

Principle Number Seven

To achieve greatness, surrender ambition.

———◆———

*W*hen you make a commitment to living life fully, you clear away reactive, fear-driven motivation and uncover the roots of your own authentic vitality. Being inspired is your natural state. Your vitality strengthens every time you give yourself permission to pay attention to the deep-rooted things you care about. This deep attunement is the natural source of enthusiasm, a word that in its original Greek means "to be filled with God." When you go about your real business—the growth of your character and spirit—success is a by-product: what happens to you along the way while you are fulfilling your true human potential. Do this, and you will not only find that you have sufficient energy to nurture yourself, but you will overflow with love for others. You will no longer approach every occasion by asking what you can get; instead, you will cherish every opportunity to give.

According to Chinese tradition, Lao Tzu's disciples were travelling through a forest one day where hundreds of trees had been cleared. In the center was one huge tree with many branches. Woodcutters rested in its shade.

The disciples asked the woodcutters why the tree had been left standing.

"Because it is absolutely useless. The bark is so tough, it breaks our saws. And even if we are able to chop off a piece, the smoke it makes when we burn it stings our eyes."

When the disciples reported this conversation to Lao Tzu, he laughed.

"Be like this tree. Be absolutely useless. If you become useful, somebody will come along and make a chair out of you. Be like this tree and you will be left alone to grow big and full, and thousands of people will come to rest under your shade."

When you are fully alive, you do not need to push or prod yourself and those around you to succeed. You have no more need of ambition than does a plant bursting through the soil towards the sun.

In this principle, you find the only cure of judging yourself by the opinions of others. Rewards and acknowledgement become irrelevent. You no longer worry if you are wasting your time or if your achievements will be recognized. Your energy is freed to contribute and create.

You remember where we left off in the story about the uneaten coffee cake—how our employees began filing in one by one to give notice? Let me tell you what happened next. After six months, the defections stopped. We looked at what was left. Miraculously, our business had undergone a self-selected pruning. The personnel and clients who resigned had been those very individuals who persisted in thinking of work as a battlefield. Interestingly enough, we had not had to fire them. They left on their own accord to join other companies who were as similarly invested in old ways of working as we had once been. Many of them have done well, advancing in their careers.

But now let me tell you about the four employees out of twenty-three who stayed—and the three clients out of fourteen! When the chips landed, these were the people who understood what we were trying to do. Upon this inspired base of support, we could begin anew. We would build a company based on a system of beliefs and behaviors that would nurture all of us in ways that the old construction never could. Continuing to draw on our credit line, we consoled ourselves that even if we were being left on the vine longer than we would have preferred, it was because we had not yet ripened fully. In God's time, not ours, we affirmed.

It took a full year. But there came a time when our little company was once again solvent. Having been forged into teamwork by the fires of crises, we had no need to form competitive, warring bands jockeying for things like better offices. There were no secret negotiations about who was going to leave with which clients. At first, we barely broke even. Then we started to make a profit. In fact, before long, our committed team of four proved to be capable of handling as much business as had been previously worked by our staff of twenty-three! We were working less and achieving more.

How enthusiasm will express itself may be very different from time to time in the span of your life. Your path will likely take unpredictable new turns. You may recognize that you've been hiding in an outgrown career and courageously choose to take some well-earned time-out to pursue something as privately passionate as planting a vegetable garden. On the other hand, you may recognize that you've beaten a retreat to spiritual pursuits in order to avoid dealing with fears of failure—and reenter the world with renewed passion.

Some of you will find the shedding of old jobs and relationships liberating. Others will find the willingness to make a commitment to staying put to be life's greatest adventure. You may discover within you a deep caring about the planet and the people on it, giving altruistic activities precedence over your history of self-gratification. Or you may discover that your efforts to save the world stem primarily from your desire to feed your ego. Unfortunately, espousing high aspirations is no guarantee that you are a superior manifestation of the lifeforce.

I learned this lesson as a result of my twentieth high school reunion not long enough ago. To say that I was feeling magnanimous is, I suppose, an understatement. My ego was still basking in the afterglow of a big write-up in a national newspaper, which had nicknamed me "the caped crusader of struggling superwomen." Capital "S" shined up for the reunion, I swept through the crowd, bestowing greetings upon the little people of my class.

The sweetest moment came when I spied, standing alone in the hallway, my nemesis from senior year. I couldn't help but notice that compared to me, in my opinion, he did not look good.

Back when we were budding journalists vying for the editorship of the *New Trier News*, the competition between us had been fierce. The publication board came up with what they thought would be an ideal solution: He and I would be named co-editors.

We were advised of the idea separately. Would I be willing to share the editorship?

Frankly, I could barely stand to be in the same room with him. But being sweet sixteen and a former Girl Scout to boot, I said, "Sure." My nemesis, when asked the same question, volunteered that if he were forced to share the job with me, he would quit.

When it finally came time for the banquet announcing the positions, parents and friends gathered, breathlessly awaiting the appointments.

I lost. He took the reins of the paper while I languished a step down on the masthead. But even as the applause for my nemesis still rang in my ears, I knew I'd been launched into a greater destiny. I was innocence clenched in a battle with the dark side. I, the bearer of the standards for all that is virtuous, good, and brave, was locked in an eternal dance with selfishness and greed. Someday, fate would rectify this grave setback.

Twenty years later, I faced him again for the first time. He was not the force of mythic proportions I remembered. No, here was the shrunken wizard himself, emerging from behind memory's fearsome facade.

He'd seen the article about me, he offered.

He was rumpled, slumped in the shoulders as he filled me in on his ups and downs of the intervening years. While I quietly basked in his seeming misfortunes, fate was at work behind the scenes, for both of us.

He told me he had been working on a novel for some time. He had no idea if it was any good or how it would be received.

I left the reunion feeling vindicated, a painful chapter of my life come to its bittersweet conclusion and the balance of the forces of good and evil rightfully restored.

Or so I thought.

Not long after my own book was published to a small but devoted following, his novel came out. Its title: *Presumed Innocent*, one of the biggest books of the decade. My nemesis: none other than author Scott Turow.

Scott's book, substantiated by millions of dollars in hardcover, paperback, and movie rights sales, is a brilliant tour de force, exposing with unprecedented candor the dark side of humanity. There is unholy sex, there is murder, there is jealousy, greed, and deception, and every manner of evil.

With this book and his subsequent efforts on racks across America, I have no place to hide from the inevitable ironies of fate. My ambition to be the ultimate good turned on me. I was forced—at last—to look beyond the moral rectification I felt I was owed by fate. Instead, I finally asked the question I had put off for more than two decades.

What did Scott have that I wanted so badly?

When I explored this question in depth, I came to some startling realizations. It wasn't really the fame he had garnered. I had achieved my cherished goal of appearing on the *Today* show and *Oprah*, discovering to my surprise that I felt less like the celebrated guest I'd fantasized myself to be and more like a product packaged into hard-selling soundbites designed to make the commercials look good.

It wasn't the money, either.

I finally admitted it was the sense that Scott could continue to romp on the dark side, while I sacrificed so much of myself—my honesty, my integrity, my authenticity— in order to be "good." I had held so much of myself in abeyance so many times in the years since then, in order to live up to inflated images I had constructed of myself sometime during my childhood.

What would a fuller expression of myself entail? How did I really want to live my life?

My first indication of what the fully lived life might look like came during an art and spirituality workshop. With the assignment for each of us to create a self-portrait of our spirits with the materials on hand, the group went to work. A groundcloth had been spread out before us, stocked lavishly with yarns, feathers, beads and fur.

Determined to experiment with authenticity, I sat immobilized as I awaited inspiration. With good intentions to tune into my inner voice, I could not help but notice that

several of the attendees had rushed the groundcloth, grabbing for the fluffiest yarns, shiniest beads, and longest
feathers. In the time it took to blink my eyes, all the pinks,
purples, whites, and yellows had been snapped up. What
was left in the rapidly diminishing pile was a whole lot of
black, red, and brown. I was angry!

I'd paid for this chance to learn to give fuller expression to my authentic self, and all I could think were the
blackest thoughts. And then I realized how perfect this
was. There was, after all, plenty of black in the pile.
Wasn't my anger authentic, too?

I took some black yarn and began winding it around
a frame made of sticks, like an intense spider weaving her
dark web. Out of the corner of my eye, I saw a gentle
friend sew the finishing touches on her portrait: a dream
blend of lovely pastels, glimmering like angel wings above
the clouds.

I grabbed red out of the pile, to vent the jealousy that
welled up in me.

Back and forth I went, between red and black, black
and red. And then, as the skein of dark passions came to
an abrupt end, I realized that I was so inside the process
of creation, my experience had transformed. In fact, a
feeling of quiet joy had crept in while I was looking the
other way. Magically, the woman with the pastel creation
chose just that moment to return her excess materials to
the groundcloth. Suddenly, I had the entire spectrum of
colors and textures available to me, weaving the many
moods and emotions that swirled through the process of
my creation into my self-portrait. There were free
oranges, subtle peaches, and vibrant blues.

The process was free and exciting—a synthesis of all
that I am: the dark energies as well as the light. As it
unfolded, I did not stop to think much about whether my

object was pretty, whether it would meet with awe and approval. The few times I did, I threw that fear and desire into the vibrant assemblage as well. I used everything. I was ruthless. I was inspired!

The forces at play in our lives are so much greater than our limited perspectives can understand. We aim for perfection, but the lifeforce battles our efforts to contain and control, and bursts forth in new creation. There is no safety in this, for the energy of life is both creative and destructive.

At birth—enduring the narrow canal to burn our lungs with our first breath of air—we instinctively understand this. We each contain the memory of what it means to be fully alive. But the memory dims. The process of growing up teaches us to surrender to the system to which we were born. We give up authentic expression for acceptance, continuing the sacrifice long after our survival is in question.

But it is that long-buried memory of being fully alive that continues to stir our discontent. The restlessness moves us to buy bigger houses, lease fancier cars, push ourselves towards the next promotion. We can stop now, giving up our quest for perfect control to take up the greater challenge of giving ourselves permission to be more fully who we already are.

In the tarot deck, there is a card called The Hermit. Alfred Douglas, in his classic book *The Tarot*, describes him as "an old man who moves slowly along a dim and stony road. He is dressed in garments resembling those of a monk. The way before him is poorly lighted by a lantern which he carries in his right hand, shielded by his sleeve from the force of the wind."

He is the archetypal symbol of the quest for meaning. The way is lonely and he has only the light of his own intuition to help him find the right path.

"To essay such an adventure takes considerable courage," Douglas says, "for by abandoning conventional values in favor of the dictates of his inner self he is setting himself apart from the comforts and authority of society in order to follow a lonely road that leads he knows not where. The Hermit illustrates a crisis of will which must be met and overcome by anyone who would advance beyond the common pale."

We cry out for peace and comfort, but The Hermit forces us to confront the bittersweet truth that spiritual maturity may march us, often against our wishes, to places we'd rather not go. The better question is not, "What can I do to be successful?" but rather, "How do I do what's right?"

What are you being called to do?

Are you willing to listen to your heart, take risks, and come to stand for something greater than yourself? Will you rise to the occasion when called, even if you have no assurance that things will turn out according to your preferences? You may make enemies, you may make sacrifices, and yet you must do what you can. You matter. What happens to you matters. You have an important job to do. Only you can do it.

The challenge of The Hermit is summarized in this quote by the philosopher Schopenhauer: "Life may be compared to a piece of embroidery, of which, during the first half of his time, a man gets a sight of the right side, and during the second half, of the wrong. The wrong side is not so pretty as the right, but it is more instructive; it shows the way in which the threads have been worked together."

When you can come to appreciate the "wrong" side of the cloth from which you have woven your life, you will be inspired. If you are unaware of the capacity for inspiration in yourself, it is because you are looking for something grand. Inspiration is simple but pervasive. You will recognize the meaning of your life when you give yourself permission to meet yourself as you are.

One of my friends, Sylvia, was a talented vocalist. Her parents had always loved opera, and were delighted that their little girl had the potential to develop into what they believed to be the star of the musical world: a coloratura soprano. They paid for her lessons, and upon graduation, Sylvia began in earnest to pursue a career in opera.

While Sylvia was always passionate about her singing, her struggle to make it her career was coupled with stress, effort, and strain. She was seen as a light-weight in the musical circles she longed to join. After several years looking for a break, she gave up.

When I bumped into her, she was doing the books for her husband's business. She loved her family life, but felt frustrated and guilty about the derailment of her career. In fact, she had given up singing entirely. The memories were just too painful.

And yet, she noted with a touch of ironic humor, she still scanned audition notes.

One day, an announcement caught her eye. The orchestra chorus was looking for vocalists. This was not a bid for the operatic stardom that had in childhood seemed her destiny. But she decided to call "for the heck of it," feeling certain that they would not need a coloratura soprano.

The secretary who answered the phone affirmed her suspicion. They did not need a soprano in the highest ranges. But they did need someone who sang mezzo. Sylvia declined, explaining her background. Rather than accept her demurral, the secretary got the choir director on the line. They were in dire need of a mezzo: Wouldn't she be willing to give it a try? By agreeing to try, she thought that perhaps she could assuage her guilt about her abandoned career without having to put anything important on the line. Certainly she was not a mezzo.

Thus defended, she arrived for her first audition in years. The accompaniest sounded the first notes of a simple piece from the mezzo repertoire. Sylvia's voice sounded thick. She threw her hands up and started to leave, but the choir director stopped her and urged her to try again.

She felt her face flush at the embarassment of not only this failure—but all her failures. The piano started up again. Struggling with the new terrain of the mezzo range, Sylvia began to cry. She stopped again.

This time the director said, even more firmly, "Keep singing." For several minutes, she alternated between crying and singing as something inside her that she had long ago tamed turned wild again. Through the tears, it became apparent to all that her voice was relaxing into the lower ranges with a richness and fullness she had not experienced in song since the unstructured days of her childhood, before the serious training began. Sylvia, in truth, had always been a mezzo. Her parent's aspirations for her had blinded her to the truth. In the middle ranges, she was anything but a lightweight. She was offered the position on the spot.

Before every performance, Sylvia takes a moment to remember. It wasn't only her willingness to sing despite her pain, her failure, and her insecurity that had liberated her authentic voice, but it was her willingness to sing with her pain and her insecurity—to give expression to all of her life's experiences.

The Sufi tradition has simple wisdom to guide us: Trust and allow your doing to become a prayer.

It is possible for you not to trust the universe and still be doing. This is, in fact, the destructive nature of our contemporary workplace. You can also trust the universe and be lazy. But if you trust the universe and remain a doer, you will be an instrument of the lifeforce. Your process will be the process of the lifeforce. Your manifestations and results will be no less than lifeforce manifesting through you.

Affirmation

I am willing to do what's next, trusting that when I follow the dictates of my heart, I am fully alive.

Conclusion

*Forgive your limitations and get on with
your life.*

When we left Sylvia, she had just been offered a
job as a mezzo in the orchestra choir. What do
you think happened next?

A. She accepted and distinguished herself as the finest
   mezzo in the state. When we last spoke, she had
   just been offered a starring role in the upcoming
   opera season.
B. She accepted and thoroughly enjoyed singing again.
   But she hadn't taken into account how much time it
   would take away from her family. Performing one
   season was a completion for her. She left her career
   at last, without remorse or regret.
C. She accepted. As it turns out, she got her greatest
   joy sharing her life experiences with younger choir
   members. After a few years, she quit the choir and
   began giving singing lessons to young girls.

The answer you guessed will tell you more about yourself
than it will about Sylvia. For when we last spoke, all of the
above were possible. Sylvia had accepted the position and
in short order had descended from elation to confusion.
There were things she loved about her new life and things

she missed. There were opportunities opening up, but there were costs. It was the same willingness to experience all of her feelings that helped Sylvia land the job that now served her through this transition.

"You see, I always thought that when I emerged from the void, it would be into something whole and specific. Now I realize that I'm emerging whole—and into a void. I don't know what the future will bring," Sylvia told me over the phone, her voice thick with emotion.

"No wonder you're upset!" I replied. "It sounds scary."

"No, you don't understand! I'm crying because I'm so afraid I might forget this feeling. I finally understand that I've got every possibility open to me. I can't wait to find out how it all turns out."

Do you hope that Sylvia becomes a star? She took a risk going to the audition and letting herself be vulnerable. Is her reward riches, glory, and fame? Is this how you will know that Sylvia is a success?

As you undoubtedly know by now, there can be a big difference between what looks to other people like you have "made it"—and your own inner experience.

This reminds me of advice given to me by a limousine driver, hired by my first publisher to chauffeur me through a demanding day of interviews with the media in New York. At the time, I was hoping that my appearances would push my book onto the top of the best-seller list and that I would be a success. Afraid I was blowing it, missing opportunities to make clever points, I felt my television makeup running down my cheeks in big, black streaks.

The driver, an elderly man who ate a salami sandwich curbside while I went on TV, looked at me crumpled in the back seat.

He'd seen them all, he commented, and they are all the same.

"They?" I understood from the tone in his voice that the "they" he was talking about included me.

"You all come here, thinking you're going to swallow this city whole. Why? It's full of snakes. You want a belly full of snakes? You want my advice. Take your best bite fast—and get the hell out."

I took his advice, and now I am usually content to add my two cents when and where I can. I no longer try to force my ideas on others. I make them available. If I can counterbalance even one moment of craziness with a little common sense, I figure I've done well for the day.

When you do receive external recognition for your achievements, it can be tempting to become overidentified with your product or position. For some, performing at your job may be the only place you feel alive. Is this inspiration or addiction? If you're not sure, see what happens when things go wrong. In this day and age, you would be foolish to count on your job, your company, or even your industry to be there for you unchanged for the duration of your career. Wouldn't it be wise for you to develop skills and resources you can call upon in times of transition? Perhaps today's heroism asks of us to embark upon the journey to discover what it means to be not just on fire with work, but with life? What good is success if you never stop long enough to check in on what shape your personal relationships are in? Can you hang out with family and friends, feeling love even if it rains on your picnic? How is your relationship with yourself? Do you feel good about your level of integrity? Do you contribute to communities of support that would be there for you—as you are willing to be there for others? Could you survive disappointment and not become a victim?

As you recover the health of your internal systems, you will no longer need to throw ambition to anxiety like a bone to a demanding dog. You will no longer fear the revelation of the vulnerability you have secretly harbored, and so you can no longer be held the emotional hostage of bosses, clients, or subordinates.

Follow the dictates of your heart, and you may well find yourself working less and achieving more. You can always hope for both the experience of success and comfort. For some, the two do coincide. But the truth is that for many of us, fulfillment of our vision may require sacrifices.

One day, not long ago, a poet turned to her wise aunt, sharing a painful moment. For years, she had poured her heart into a book of poems that had just been rejected by the twentieth publisher.

"I thought that if you courageously peel away the façade and take big risks by expressing your authentic self openly, the money will come."

Her aunt quietly poured another cup of lemonade.

"Dear niece," she said, "it is more likely to turn out that way when you peel down to the core and find that your authentic self contains an investment banker inside."

You get into difficulty when you confuse your potential to have unlimited vision with the childlike belief that you have unlimited means, as well.

As psychologist Rollo May points out in his classic book *Freedom and Destiny*, devoid of limitation, we would be like a river without banks. Our genetic, historic, emotional, and spiritual legacies give our life velocity. And even as we are propelled downstream, we are always free to make the best possible choice under the circumstances. Each of us has those things in our past and our makeup that work for and against us. For example, you may have more brains but somebody else has family connections.

He may have family money but lacks your creative spunk. Who will garner the greatest experience of success in life? All of us have strengths and weaknesses. But are our weaknesses really the problem?

Even if you don't feel passionate about your job you can still choose to feel passionate about your life. Enthusiasm is catching. Let it begin anywhere, and watch with amazement as even the most resistant timber catches fire. You can begin by taking baby steps to what's next. E-mail a long lost friend. Treat yourself to the rarest cheese on the shelf. Practice your golf swing while the copier prints out. Take every opportunity to crack open your façade of old beliefs and habits and let the humor, openness, perspective, and faith jump out. Use your very life as fuel, and trust that the fire in your heart is transforming the inner experience of what it means to be a success. As you do, the heat and warmth you are producing will attract new opportunities for greatness beyond what you had imagined.

Perhaps doing what's next will bring you to a time and place that calls for heroism on a grand public scale. Perhaps your moment of heroism is quiet and internal. It is heroic to find as much time in your life as you can muster to love your children, your spouse, your friends, or to create for the sheer ecstasy of self-expression. For some, the experience of success you seek will be found after your own workday is ended, serving others as they go through the line at the local soup kitchen.

So what if our jobs do not supply us with the outlet for creative expression, social life, meaningful contribution, and sufficient money to impress our friends that we grew up thinking they would? The search for the rewards we have been taught we deserve for our good behavior has taken us from position to position, job to job, career to career.

But no boss, no work environment, no career can fill the emptiness where the universe's end of the bargain—the promise that if we were good enough we could have it all—was supposed to be.

When we embark upon the path of inner excellence, we stop wasting energy trying to make our workplaces perform at the behest of our childhood fantasies. Instead, we are grateful for what work does do: It provides us with the means to support our lives, and the lives of those we care for. Because you know you have a roof over your head tonight and food on the table, you can, if you so choose, be among the privileged few on this planet who can move beyond issues of personal survival and begin to explore expanded dimensions of what it means to be fully alive.

You may discover that you have less of a need for material things. But you don't need to throw away everything you've worked for, either. There is no guarantee that giving away all your possessions and going to sit on a mountaintop will take you to peace and fulfillment any faster than would staying in your old job and experimenting with new ways of working.

Rabbi Nathan Segal told his Marin County congregation the story of a seeker of wisdom. The seeker had heard of a spiritual master who had spent decades atop a sacred mountain, discovering the secret to happiness.

The seeker set out to find this master, risking his life to cross frozen fields of snow, climb barren foothills, hang from cliffs—finally to arrive at the master's feet.

"Master! I have come all this way. Tell me. What is the secret of happiness?"

The master took a deep breath and then stated:

"It's the sunset."

"The sunset?" the seeker asked increduously.

The master paused a moment, then responded, "It's not the sunset?"

When you are grounded in inner excellence, nobody but you can judge the meaning of your life. You can't tell anything from appearances. Consider this. When you look at a tree in late summer, the leaves are abundantly lush and green. But what is really going on? Even as the leaves rustle in the breeze, the trunk and limbs are shutting down for the winter. Now take another look at our tree towards the end of winter. Now the tree looks dead. But what is really going on? New sap is bursting with life just beneath the bark. Just as you cannot judge a tree by appearance alone, so should you refrain from judging yourself by how your external circumstances appear to others. Only you can know the truth about what is birthing in you. Have compassion for yourself and forgive your work for its limitations and get on with your life.

When you give up resentment, even simple tasks can hold fulfillment. A Zen master, encountering a teacher putting the finishing touchs on the monastery's remodeled kitchen, asked how things were going.

"Everything's going fine," the teacher answered. "There are only a few details to finish up."

Upon hearing this, the master scratched his head.

"Only a few details? But details are all there are."

You are afraid your status in life does not reflect your full potential? Work, no matter how mundane, can provide the opportunity to nurture your character and spirit. You can practice teamwork, compassion, discipline, and responsiveness. Haven't you ever noticed that you can walk into one fast food outlet and everybody seems angry and resentful? Go next door, and it's an entirely different story. At the fast food restaurant just down the street, everybody is smiling. The cashier is pleasant and attentive. The salaries and benefits are the same. The food offerings are nearly identical. But in the first, the manager feels that the job is beneath her. In the second, the boss is grateful to have the opportunity to serve.

Ironically, at the very moment we stop demanding that our careers deliver success to us, we find ourselves attracting those who want what we now have: the ability to operate in support of life, not out of fear. Those who were previously able to engage us in their reward and punishment-driven games of power fall away. When our spirit is strong, we repel those who once fed off our denial. We stop taking abuse from clients, bosses, and subordinates and start to demand respect—and we stop passing the abuse along.

If, as a result, we are in a position to take a new job or hire a new employee, we can seek out people to work with who complement not only our skills but our visions. The strength and stability of our companies reflect the degree to which we can support each other to bring our values and our spirits to work with us each day. You turn your workplace into sacred space when you become willing to care for one another, not manipulate each other to serve selfish purposes. You take the leap of faith to think of your work as a calling, the opportunity for you to do your part in creating an environment in which others can also make their contribution to the greater good.

The work of transforming our experience of business from fear to life begins with these principles. But the internal work prescribed in this book is only the beginning. Over the coming decades, as managers develop sufficient inner strength, the overflow will transform our workplaces. Released from the carrot and the stick, few of us will want to continue the sixty- or seventy-hour weeks that have become the norm.

When we work to live, rather than live to work, we realize that should we choose to limit the hours we work each week, we can leave enough time to nurture other important aspects of our lives. When we give ourselves time to refresh and revitalize, we return to work with our entire capacity to contribute renewed and available.

The creative options for cultivating and revitalizing ourselves and the people in our workplaces are as unlimited as the human imagination—from flex-time to increased vacations, from allowing time for reflection in the workday without reprimand to cutting out enforced overtime.

An increasing number of companies are experimenting with new ways of working that take into consideration the whole person's needs through all life stages, such as on-site daycare, paternity as well as maternity leaves, sabbaticals. In the age of the global economy, coupled with dramatic demographic shifts, the corporation of the future will need leaders who can work interpersonally with employees of many cultures, ages, and educational backgrounds. The challenges of the future will cause managers to call upon inner resources as never before. Those who will have the competitive advantage are the very people who have taken the time to do the challenging inner work prescribed in this book. The external and the internal will converge in the simple realization destined to change the way we do business in this country: Inspired people do inspired work.

The Chinese philosopher Chuang Tzu tells the story of Ch'ing, the chief carpenter of ancient China, who took on the task of carving a music stand out of wood for the imperial court. So superlative was Ch'ing's work that upon finishing, all those who saw it exclaimed that it must be of supernatural origin.

"What secret is there in your art?" asked Prince Lu.

"No secret, Your Highness," replied Ch'ing. "And yet there is something. When I am about to make such a stand, I quiet my mind and guard against any diminution of my spirit.

"Three days in this condition, and I become oblivious of any reward to be gained.

"Five days, and I forget about any fame to be acquired.

"Then, when there is no thought of the court present in my mind, my skill becomes concentrated, and all disturbing elements from without are gone. Then I enter some mountain forest, searching for a suitable tree. When I find the right tree, I can see the stand in my mind's eye. Then I set to work.

"Beyond that, there is nothing. I bring my own native capacity into relation with that of the wood. What was suspected to be of supernatural execution in my work is due solely to this."

We are pioneers poised on the brink of yet another frontier: the human spirit. Seen from this new perspective, the true task of the individual is to rise to his or her own highest level of development as a human being, inspiring others to do the same.

Allen, an account supervisor at an advertising agency in San Francisco, came a long way to become such an explorer. Landing a major baby food company as a client, Allen was quick to let his staff know that "there would be no room for mistakes." He never took vacations, working nights and weekends "in case something came up."

' He was hooked on being in control — but the price was enormous.

Staff turnover was one problem. But the bigger problem was that constantly going on overdrive, he was forced to do everything the hard and long way. He was cut off from the very inspiration and creativity that had won him the business in the first place. As long as things went well, Allen was in great form. But when things didn't go exactly his way, he could not regain equilibrium without the benefit of increasingly large glasses of wine. Before long, the man who never wanted to leave anything to chance was forced to take an extended leave of absence at a treatment center.

While there, Allen had to let go of his job, surrendering to the ebbs and tides of his recovery. Ironically, in his absence, his division thrived. Freed from the frenetic, fear-driven pace, they began to produce higher quality work. Upon his return, Allen vowed to practice the principles of inner excellence, paying attention to the growth of his own character and spirit and creating an environment that supported the staff. By the end of the year, his division had transformed into one of the healthiest in the company. Allen observes that the more he had surrendered control, the more his division and life thrived.

When you commit yourself to confronting the truth, trusting that you can bring compassion to whatever you discover, you will flow into what's next for you. You won't need to push or control the outcome. You will sacrifice the illusion that you can bribe fate with your good behavior — but you will receive, in return, the gift of partnership with the divine.

The challenge of our generation of leadership is to cut through the tyranny of the illusion of control and expand our definition of success to center on spiritual qualities that run counter to the precepts of contemporary business philosophy. The irony is that by doing what seems diametrically opposed to our notion of what it takes to succeed, we find the only path that leads to an experience of success that can endure.

There is an old Persian story about a young man who stumbled upon a mountain cave. Peering cautiously inside, he spied a priceless pearl clasped in the claws of a fierce dragon. The boy plotted and planned, but eventually gave up trying to retrieve the pearl. He reconciled himself to living an ordinary life.

Over the years, he got a job. He married and had children. He lived his everyday life, forgetting about the pearl until he was very old. Then one day, he remembered.

Taking up his walking stick, he hobbled to the cave. To his amazement, the pearl was still there. But even more astonishing, the dragon had shrunk to the size of a harmless lizard. The old man easily picked up the pearl and carried it away. The fierce battle that he'd plotted in his youth had been won inside himself as he met the challenges of his daily life. It was he who had grown in inner strength and stature.

You can redefine success for yourself, experiencing fulfillment whatever the "facts" of your career appear to be at any given time. You can replace ambition with purpose, fueling your actions by inspiration rather than fear. Ultimately, as my company did, you can allow your greatest success to come as a by-product of who you have become.

On the path prescribed by the Seven Principles of Inner Excellence, there are no deadends. Every moment, you are free to make the choice that will help you to fulfill your purpose the most direct way possible. When you begin to act, the action changes you as you find resources inside of you that you did not know you had. You make space for a power greater than yourself to become engaged in your life. You are, at last, fully alive.

These seven principles worked for me. Believe and they will work for you, too.

Appendix

Group Study Guide

Inner Excellence at Work lends itself to either individual or group study. The following exercises and discussion questions are designed to help you work through the subject matter of the Seven Principles of Inner Excellence, one session at a time.

Many groups prefer to meet once a week for twelve weeks, considering one section of the book each week. One hour a week is sufficient, but each week's material could easily expand to fill two or more hours. Feel free to experiment with one- or two-day retreats, twelve consecutive evenings, or any other format that suits your needs.

In the suggested twelve-session format, you may wish to assign group members to read the introductory material up to the beginning of chapter one prior to the first gathering. During the subsequent eleven sessions, you will work through each of the chapters and principles in turn. (It is helpful if the group comes prepared, having read that week's section.)

Depending on the length and interest of the group, you may want to spend more time on some questions and exercises, and less on others. Feel free to select and adapt the suggestions to your own group's needs and desires.

Week I: Preface—Finding Meaning and Success in a Changing World

Discussion Questions

1. What are some of the success advice books (or motivational speakers or courses) you've turned to over the years that gave the message that to get what you want, all you have to do is work harder, smarter, longer than the next guy or company? Did their advice work? If not, why not?
2. Do you think the workplace as a whole has gotten "meaner" or "tougher" since you first went to work? Why? Are there any benefits to this? What has been lost?
3. Is there a qualitative difference between ambition that is being fueled by inspiration or by fear? Can you know whether somebody else's motivations are inspired or fear-driven, or is this something you can only know about yourself? What are some of the clues that tip you off? (Please note that these questions—and all of the questions to come—do not need to be resolved, individually or as a group. What is important is that your feelings and opinions—as well as those of others—be noted and welcomed.)

Exercises

1. What does *inner excellence* mean to you? If there is a dictionary nearby, look each of these words up. (In several dictionaries, if possible.) Do you agree with the definitions? Do you have a different idea? Take the time to formulate your own definition of *inner excellence* and then share it with the group.

2. Write a letter expressing your feelings to an author or individual in your life who promised you that if only you work harder, smarter, and longer than the next guy or company, you will succeed. At the conclusion, decide what, if anything, to do with the letter. (For this and all future exercises, you may want to use quiet background music to help create a reflective atmosphere.)

Week II: Chapter One—The Discovery of Inner Excellence

Discussion Questions

1. Would you make a good candidate for Overachievers Anonymous?
2. What is the difference between hard work driven by passion and hard work driven by desperation? Can you tell by somebody's results which is fueling their ambition? Which source of motivation is likelier to lead to burn-out?
3. Are exhaustion and burn-out primarily signs of personal weakness or imperfection, or does our society as a whole bear responsibility?

Exercises

1. Think of someone who is commonly thought of as one of the most powerful businesspeople in the country. (For example, Bill Gates, Donald Trump, or Leona Helmsley.) Create two columns: one marked "virtues," the other marked "vices." Now brainstorm the personal qualities or characteristics that you identify with this individual. Are there

more virtues than vices or visa versa? If you are doing this with a group, is there debate concerning whether any particular qualities are virtues or vices? At the conclusion, discuss why you think our society as a whole admires this individual?

2. Bring in some tabloids and ask the group to flip through looking for stories about celebrities that portray them as "having it all." Realistically, how could there be time for all the career responsibilities and idealized parenting/relationship involvements to be happening simultaneously in that celebrity's life? Pick one of the most obvious examples of someone who appears to have it all, and based on what you read and surmise, do a mock daily schedule of your idea of what you think one typical day of this person's life must look like. (Use an actual page from an appointment book, if possible.) Don't forget to set aside time for this individual to have make-up and hair done, shop for clothes, stay in top-notch physical condition, make charity appearances, and so on. Can you fit it all in? Is there still time for this person to sleep?

Week III: Chapter Two—Life-Driven Work

Discussion Questions

1. In the story of the chicken and the pig, which animal do you identify with more? Which animal's approach would make the greater contribution to the workplace in the short-run? Over time?

2. Do you agree that at some point, working harder and longer can become counterproductive?

3. This chapter states that "we are all spiritual beings." Do you agree with this? Is it alright to be spiritual outside of places of worship? Where is the line drawn between personal spirituality and proselytization?

Exercises

1. What other metaphors besides work as warfare could you use to describe your career or worklife? Write or draw a description of a metaphor for work that makes better sense for you. (If a more positive metaphor cannot be found to describe your current work situation, find a metaphor for your ideal workplace.)
2. Bring in a stack of business magazines and flip through them, looking for examples of advertisements (and editorial copy) that portray rushing around, anxiety, self-sacrifice, and the like as glamorous or desirable. Why do you think these images sell products?

Week IV: Chapter Three—Reclaiming Our Human Resources

Discussion Questions

1. Do you think Autry's ideal manager would succeed or fail in your workplace? Why?
2. In what ways, if any, has your workplace (or others you may have read or heard about) reduced anxiety and created a nurturing environment for the people who work there? If you can't answer this for a company as a whole, do you know individuals who

have been able to improve the quality of life at work for themselves or those with whom they work?

3. Make a list of all the industries you can think of that are currently struggling or in trouble. Pick one with which you are familiar. Does that industry's culture tend to value or undermine the vitality of the individuals who work within it? Is it possible for an individual to be vital and healthy despite working within a destructive environment?

Exercises

1. Pretend that you are entrepreneurs wanting to present your business idea to a group of possible investors. This group of investors have the aspiration of funding companies that not only make money, but that create a positive working environment for their employees. Work on teams to develop as detailed a presentation as possible to present to the group. (You can pick the actual industry you are already in or you can agree to work on any industry or work situation that interests you. Here's one suggestion: a new bottled water company with aspirations to sell not only the highest quality water in the market, but to do so with integrity and quality of life for everyone affiliated.) Each team presents their ideas to the group. At the conclusion, vote to see who will get the capital.

2. Write a Personal Mission Statement. To begin, complete these first three statements in writing:

    I believe the skills, character, spirit, and attributes I have to contribute are: _____. I am pleased when I have the opportunity to use these qualities to:_____.
    The ideal impact I believe I could have on the world around me through the expression of these qualities is: _____.

After you've completed this first part of the exercise, combine your ideas into one statement which expresses your sense of your life work or purpose. Take time to condense and refine it so that it says exactly what you want your life and work to be about.

Week V: Principle One—Change your beliefs about the nature of business and of life, and you will change how you manage your career.

Discussion Questions

1. Do you do your best work in an environment of fear or one of trust? Do you think this is true of most people?
2. Do you agree that there can be some benefits to experiencing irresolution and pain? What are some of these benefits? What are some of the ways you could avoid experiencing irresolution and pain? Is this healthy?
3. Does your faith tradition or spiritual orientation have anything to say about surrendering control? (Remember, particularly if you are in an interfaith context, these questions are about sharing information, not trying to convince others to abandon their beliefs for yours.) Why do you think so many traditions consider surrendering control to a higher power as a spiritual key?

Exercises

1. Reread the section in this chapter in which individuals at a blues bash share their fear-based beliefs. Revisit each belief, rating on a scale of

1 to 5 (five being the highest) how big a part that particular belief plays in your life. On a blank piece of paper, make a list of any belief that you rated 3 or higher. What other negative beliefs do you hold that weren't mentioned in this section of the book? Write these down as well. When you are done, put your lists in a pile and shuffle them around. Ask everyone to pick one list out of the pile. Then, break into teams to put on improvised skits for each other. Imagine that your team is seated together at a table at a blues bash having a conversation about what it takes to succeed at work. Your dialogue is based on the list you have chosen from the stack. Say your lines with feeling and see if you can have some fun with this.

2. Take the list of negative beliefs you chose from the pile and dispose of them in some way. One suggestion is to crush the paper into balls and see who can toss theirs into the trashcan from farthest away.

Week VI: Principle Two—In order to become fully successful, you must first be fully alive.

Discussion Questions

1. What do you think is meant by the phrase "fully alive." Can you think of somebody who exemplifies this quality? (Can you think of somebody who, on the other hand, is "half-dead?") Are these qualities something we are born with, or can they be learned?
2. Discuss spiritual "short-cuts." What philosophies or techniques have you tried that offered the promise of perfect control over your life? Did they work? If not, why not?

Exercises

1. Hand everyone a page from a children's coloring book and some crayons. Individuals are instructed to color only outside the lines. After completion, discuss how easy or difficult this was for you. Did you find yourself resenting the limitations? Not following instructions? Or was it fun and freeing?

2. Here's another exercise concerned with relinquishing control. Choose a partner (preferably by chance, such as pulling their name from a hat) and put a blindfold on them. Lead them safely around the premises for ten minutes or so, then switch. (Go out of the room and outdoors, if possible.) How did it feel having to put your faith in someone other than yourself?

Stage VII: Principle Three—When you empty yourself of the illusion of who you thought you were, there is less to lose than you had feared.

Discussion Questions

1. One of the people quoted in this chapter suggested that instead of expanding our comfort levels, we should expand our discomfort levels. What do you think she meant by this? Do you think this is wise advice?

2. Why is there so often a discrepancy between who people think they are and how they are perceived by others? Are there advantages to minimizing the discrepancy? Why or why not? If you think it's a good thing, what do you think it would take to close the gap?

Exercises

1. Take a personal inventory. In each pair of opposing qualities, which are the words that you feel reflect your greatest strengths and weaknesses? Make two columns, one labeled "strengths," one labeled "weaknesses." Write down those words that trigger the strongest emotions for you in the appropriate column. Do not feel obligated to share the results. This is for your own information. Be as honest as possible. (Leader, read this list slowly and give people time to write down their answers.)

   Arrogant/Humble, Reactive/Stable, Anxious/Calm, Defensive/Open, Dishonest/Honest, Unreliable/Consistent, Insincere/Sincere, Indiscreet/Discreet, Self-involved/Loving, Unkind/Kind, Rude/Courteous, Argumentative/Amiable, Jealous/Content, Gossipy/Respectful, Suspicious/Trusting, Withdrawn/Enthusiastic, Grudging/Forgiving, Dominating/Collaborating, Manipulative/Straightforward, Submissive/Assertive, Irrational/Rational, Unrealistic/Realistic, Pushing/Patient, Judgmental/Constructive, Stubborn/Accommodating, Self-pitying/Reflective, Selfish/Giving, Self-centered/Caring, Desperate/Confident, Despondent/Optimistic, Guilt-ridden/Resolved, Lazy/Productive, Procrastinating/Efficient, Aimless/Directed, Irresponsible/Responsible, Ungrateful/Grateful.

   Homework: Instruct the group to revisit their Personal Mission Statement (completed in Week IV) and see if it reflects what they now believe to be their strongest attributes and qualities. Ask them to take the time to update their Personal Mission Statement, if necessary.

2. Follow the precedure outlined to Kirk in this chapter (page 73) to come up with your own affirmation.

Week VIII: Principle Four—You have the choice between being victimized by circumstances or being initiated by them.

Discussion Questions

1. Who do you know who has proven to be a resilient person, despite facing big challenges? Do you know someone who has become victimized in a big way by what you perceive to be a minor setback? (You don't need to give names.) What qualities or characteristics do each have that helped to determine how they react to obstacles in their lives? What personal qualities and characteristics best serve an individual experiencing challenges?
2. Can you think of a time in your life when you thought that you were a victim of circumstances, but in retrospect, you turned out to have a more favorable outcome than you could have imagined at the time?

Exercises

1. Think of an unresolved situation in your life as if it were a story. In fact, write the words "Once upon a time" at the top of a page and write a brief summary of the situation. When you are up to date, imagine three possible endings. (Put each ending on a separate page.) Make the first ending your fear. Make the second ending the best possible outcome.

Make your third ending something in the middle—
neither the best nor worst possible outcome. When
you are done, come up with three more positive
outcomes you hadn't previously considered. If you
need help, ask the group for suggestions. (Feel free
to discard any endings you don't want in your life.)

2. Write a letter to yourself describing how proud you
are of how well you've been doing, given who you
are, where you've come from, and the challenges
you face. Now that you have come this far, what else
would you like to bring to bear on the situation you
face in the future? Hand out stamps and actually
mail the letters to arrive at homes or workplaces.

Week IX: Principle Five—When you are driven by life, the odds will be with you.

Discussion Questions

1. Do you agree with Einstein that the most important
question every individual must ask him or herself is
whether or not this is a friendly universe? Do you
think that if things aren't going your way at any
given time, this could still be a friendly universe?
2. Share stories about lucky accidents and coincidences
in your life. What is your explanation? If you
believe in magic or miracles, are you free to talk
about your feelings and beliefs with others?

Exercises

1. Compose a prayer or invocation following the
instructions in this chapter on page 94.
2. Take out a dollar bill and see how many different
spiritual images and slogans you can find. What do

you think they mean? (A Latin dictionary or somebody who speaks Latin would be useful.) Why do you think our founding fathers chose to put them on our currency?

Week X: Principle Six—Your ordinary self is enough.

Discussion Questions

1. Reread the story about the two disciples who meet across the banks of a river told on page 110. What is so miraculous about eating when you're hungry and sleeping when you're tired? In what ways could you use the message of this story to enhance your worklife?

2. Think about your last several vacations. Were they busy or restful? When and how do you relax in the course of your daily life? What do you think prevents busy people from taking quiet time for themselves?

Exercise

1. What is your achievable dream? Ask the group to write the answers to these questions. (Give the group sufficient time to answer each segment.)

   - Five years from now, what I hope to have achieved in the area of my career or work is _____.
   - What I hope to have achieved in the area of my lifestyle/financial picture is _____.
   - What I hope to have achieved in the area of my relationships is _____.

- What I hope to have achieved in the area of community involvement is _____.
- What I hope to have achieved in the area of my physical, spiritual, and emotional health is _____.
    (Repeat the series for one year from now; six months from now; one month from now; tomorrow. i.e. "One year from now, what I hope to have achieved in the area of my career or work is _____," etc.)

2. Do you feel like you don't have a minute to spare in your life for rest and relaxation? Turns out, we all do. And furthermore, the right kind of minute is a very, long time. Take out a watch with a second hand and ask the group to sit silently for a whole minute. In anticipation of this minute, instruct the group to breathe slowly and deeply and to quiet their thoughts. One way to do this is to imagine your mind as a calm pool of water. If a thought comes, imagine it to be a pebble skipping across the surface. Watch the ripples on the pond as the surface calms back down. Tell the group when to begin and ask them to note silently when they think they've hit the minute-mark. (No fair looking at a watch.) Prepare to be surprised!

Week XI: Principle Seven— To achieve greatness, you must surrender ambition.

Discussion Questions

1. Alfred Douglas describes the Hermit as someone who "sets himself apart from the comfort and authority of society in order to follow a lonely road

he knows not where." Does this image hold any appeal for you? Do you think it would be possible to have this Hermit-quality as part of your personality and still play an active role in the work world? Are there any advantages to giving expression to this quality in your worklife?

2. Talk about ambition in relation to a child taking his/her first step. What qualities do children bring to their play, learning, and growth that you admire? When/how does ambition change into something qualitatively different? Is there any way you can incorporate some of these original qualities in your life?

Exercises

1. Commit to one activity that you can trust to fan the flame of your passion for life. It can be a baby step (i.e. doing crossword puzzles, e-mailing an old friend, tap-dancing at the copier) or it can be something major (i.e. going back to school for additional education, putting your name in for a promotion, etc.) Perhaps it will be something you used to love to do as a child. Make your commitment out loud to the group. Acknowledge each other's pledges with applause.
2. Write a letter to your job/work/career, thanking it, despite everything, for all that it has done for you.

Week XII: Conclusion

Discussion Questions

1. Do you agree with Rollo May's assessment that "devoid of limitation, we'd be like a river without banks?" What are your river banks?

2. In the story related in this chapter about the singer, Sylvia, which option did you think Sylvia chose: A, B, or C? What do you think your choice for Sylvia says about you?

3. Has your understanding of what it means to be a "success" in our society changed over the course of these sessions?

4. What personal, corporate, or community resources can you call upon in times of transition? If you can't think of whom to call upon for help on any issue, ask the group to help you brainstorm for ideas.

Exercises

1. Pick one of the invocations from the book that appeals most to you (or write your own). Make a poster out of key words or the entire invocation to post in your workspace to remind you on a daily basis of what you've learned during this series. (If you can, bring in a stack of colorful magazines and have people decorate their posters with a collage of images inspired by the invocation.)

2. Plan some kind of celebration. Perhaps a potluck snack or meal. If possible, arrange the celebration as a field trip to a favorite restaurant where you know that the people are genuinely upbeat and happy to be of service.

3. Discuss whether you'd like to continue meeting together. What questions would you like to revisit? What issues have yet to be addressed? Would you like to meet periodically just to stay in touch? If so, it's useful to plan a specific date to get together again before you officially end your studies.

For further study, you can use several of Carol Orsborn's books which lend themselves for individual or group study. *The Art of Resilience* has a ten-session study guide available. You can receive a free guide by sending a SASE to Resilience, c/o The Orsborn Company, P.O. Box 159061, Nashville, TN 37215. *Solved by Sunset* is intended as a self-guided retreat on the subject of intuitive decision making, but also lends itself to group retreats or weekly sessions. For updated information, consult Carol Orsborn's interactive Web site: www.innerexcellence.com, which will also connect you to her e-mail address for questions and comments. Carol Orsborn is also available for workshops and keynote speeches. For information, phone (615) 321-8890.

The Seven Principles of Inner Excellence

Principle Number One

*Change your beliefs about the nature of business and of life,
and you will change how you manage your career.*

Principle Number Two

*In order to become fully successful, you must first
be fully alive.*

Principle Number Three

*When you give up the illusion of who you thought you were,
there is less to lose than you had feared.*

Principle Number Four

*You have the choice between being victimized by circumstances
or being initiated by them.*

Principle Number Five

When you are driven by life, the odds will be with you.

Principle Number Six

Your ordinary self is enough.

Principle Number Seven

To achieve greatness, surrender ambition.

Seven Affirmations

1. I surrender the illusion that I can control everything that happens to me and to those I care about.

2. I am willing to embrace all that I am—including my fears, pain, and limitations as well as my loves, comforts, and happiness—realizing that in doing so, I am expanding to fulfill my true human potential.

3. I reclaim my right to authentic expression.

4. I have compassion for myself and the human condition.

5. By responding to the entreaties of my heart, I contribute to the creation of a better future than would otherwise have occurred.

6. I nurture myself at a pace supportive of my overall vitality.

7. I am willing to do what's next, trusting that when I follow the dictates of my heart, I am fully alive.

Invocations for Inner Excellence

For the Work Day

I trust that when I pay attention to the deepest
   behests of my heart,
I am being led to my greater purpose the fastest
   way possible.

If it seems long and difficult at times, it is because I
   am a beginner at this.
If I am disappointed or frustrated along the way, I
   simply make whatever corrections I can.
If I can't find anything to correct, I have the
   patience to wait.

When I am tempted to take a short-cut that I know
   does not come from my heart,
Grant me the clarity to see that imitation will
   merely give the illusion of success.
When I compare myself to others, help me to turn
   jealousy into a blessing for them, feeling grateful
   for what I, too, have achieved.
Help me to love myself, trusting that when I pay
   attention to these things—given where I've come
   from and the circumstances I face—I am always
   doing my best.

For Motivation

When practicing the Principles of Inner Excellence,
  I am motivated by inspiration not fear.
An enhanced experience of success is what happens
  for me along the way, while I'm living my life
  fully.
In order to be fully successful, I must first be fully
  alive.

For Greatness

The job I am doing now is a small part of what is in
  store for me.
The real purpose of my work is to provide a forum
  for the evolution of my character and my spirit.

When I give up my arrogance—my fascination with
  significance—I see that every day provides
  many opportunities for such greatness.
But I must remember that as I proceed, my
  experience will not be that I am doing
  something great, but merely that I am doing
  what's next.

For the Hero's Way

The bridge I am traversing from the old to the new
    is crumbling beneath my feet as I go
Knowing that there will be no turning back, help
    me to find the strength to hold on to my faith.

The price for going for what my heart is telling me
    to do at first seems always greater than what I
    am willing to pay . . . but it isn't.
Give me the strength to let go of the way things
    were, watching in awe as a better life
    reconfigures around my inner experience of
    success.

For New Beginnings

All that is truly meant to be mine will be given to
    me in time. Even if I fear I don't deserve it.
    Even if I have thrown it away.

May I remember that any moment can be a turning
    point.
I can begin anew the moment I envision the best
    rather than worst possible outcome.

For One Who Stands Alone

May I honor myself for following the dictates of my
    heart,
Understanding that I am wise enough to take into
    consideration the advice of others
Courageous enough to stand alone.

May I come to trust that responding to the
    entreaties of my heart with my best guess is
    always good enough.
And that on the only path that truly counts, the
    journey to increased wisdom, love, and
    knowledge,
There are, in truth, no dead ends.

For Risk Takers

I honor myself for my willingness to follow the
    behests of my heart,
Remembering that if there were not the potential
    for pain, there would not be risk.
Where there is no risk, there can be no growth.

For Bad Times

When the sun arrives at its new dawn, it turns
   towards its setting.
The moon when full begins to wane.
The flowering plant grows toward the sun, and
   from the weight of its own blossom bends to the
   ground and dies.

Knowing these things, may I relinquish the illusion
   of control, willing to surrender everything to the
   conditions of the time.
May I tear the sack open and throw the seeds of my
   life to the wind releasing, crying for mercy,
   feeling the pain.

May I be blessed with willingness, watching many
   seeds blow away, rejoicing for even the one that
   lands on fertile soil enriched by fallen flowers
   long past.

It will take root.

I understand that I may feel the urgency of
   resolution pressing upon me,
But grant me the patience not to force the seed to
   emerge before its time.
Rather, may I tend the bare, dark spot of earth
   diligently with patience and discipline
So it is that when the sun is at its zenith it rises
   toward a new dawn.
The moon when empty of light waxes again.
Through the dark patch of fertile soil, a seed at last
   sends up a tender shoot.
May I find it in my heart to embrace it all.

For One Who Has Failed

I am where I am and it's all right.
The goal I sought represents a commitment to a
    process.
When I fail, I replace judgment with observation.
I trust myself to correct what I can.
    Forgive myself for what I can't.

My worthiness does not depend on my
    achievements.
My worthiness is not up for question.
Knowing that there is more that I want for myself
    does not invalidate what I already have.

Regardless of how much at a standstill I feel myself
    to be,
The currents of my destiny continue to work on my
    behalf moving me forward to new opportunities
    and possibilities from which to choose.
I am ready to be surprised.

For One in Painful Transition

I find myself in a time of growth
    where I am too much for the systems that once
    contained me.
I feel so lost and alone, but my heart cries out
    to me:

"Look carefully! It is only your old constructions
    that are dying.
Of course it is painful to watch them go —
    How could you not grieve for that which was
    once so important to you?

But tell the whole truth as you grieve,
For you know that something is birthing, too."

May I loosen my grip on that which is passing away
And place my attention and energy on that which
    wants to be born.

For Inspiring Others

May I recognize that when I inspire people,
    it is not because of what I do,
    but because of who I am.

I inspire people when I share my genuine
    enthusiasm for life by listening and receiving as
    well as by giving and telling.
When I have the courage to say what needs to be
    said,
Remembering that it is my actions not my words
    that carry the message.
When I am willing to expose more of who I really
    am with trust and vulnerability,
Even when it stretches me beyond my own comfort
    level.

For the Restoration of Integrity

Shaken by the confrontation of aspects of myself I
do not like, I do my best to rectify my errors.
When I've done my best, I humbly ask for
compassion to be restored.
Not as one, saying, "Here is my authentic self. You
have to love me."
Rather, by saying, "Here is my authentic self, flaws
and all.
While I prefer you love me, I am willing to take the
consequences."

My guilt fuels my heart with resolve to do better
next time.
For I have the right to be whole again.
And being whole includes my right to make
mistakes and my right to make amends.

Bibliography

Alcoholics Anonymous. *Alcoholics Anonymous*. New York: Alcoholics Anonymous World Services, Inc., 1987.

Autry, James. *Work and Life*. New York: William Morrow, 1994.

Borysenko, Joan, Ph.D. *Pocketful of Miracles: Prayers, Meditations and Affirmations to Nurture Your Spirit Every Day of the Year*. New York: Warner Books, 1994.

Breton, Denise and Christopher Largent. *Love, Soul and Freedom: Dancing with Rumi on the Mystic Path*. Minneapolis, Minn.: Hazelden, 1998.

Campbell, Joseph, with Bill Moyers. *The Power of Myth*. New York: Doubleday, 1988.

Chodron, Pema. *Start Where You Are: A Guide to Compassionate Living*. Boston: Shambhala, 1994.

Citron, Sterna. *Why the Baal Shem Tov Laughed: Fifty-two Stories about Our Great Chasidic Rabbis*. Northvale, N.J.: Jason Aronson, Inc., 1993.

Cobb, John B., Jr. and David Ray Griffin. *Process Theology: An Introductory Exposition*. New Jersey: The Westminster Press, 1976.

Dominguez, Joe and Vicki Robin. *Your Money or Your Life*. New York: Viking/Penguin, 1993.

Douglas, Alfred. *The Tarot*. New York: Penguin, 1972.

Fields, Rick. *Chop Wood Carry Water: A Guide to Finding Spiritual Fulfillment in Everyday Life*. New York: Tarcher, 1984.

Harman, Willis, Ph.D. and John Hormann. *Creative Work*. Sausalito, Calif.: The Institute of Noetic Sciences, 1990.

Harman, Willis, Ph.D. *Global Mind Change*. Sausalito, Calif.: The Institute for Noetic Sciences, 1988.

Heschel, Abraham Joshua. *I Asked for Wonder*, edited by Samuel H. Dresner. New York: Crossroad, 1983.

Heschel, Abraham Joshua. *A Passion for Truth*. Woodstock, VT: Jewish Lights, 1995.

James, William. *The Varieties of Religious Experience: A Study in Human Nature*. Introduction by Reinhold Niebuhr. New York: Collier Books, 1961.

Johnson, Robert A. *He: Understanding Masculine Psychology*. New York: Harper and Row, 1974.

Kushner, Harold. *Who Needs God*. New York: Pocket Books, 1989.

Kuner, Susan, Carol Orsborn, Linda Quigley, and Karen Stroup. *Speak the Language of Healing*. Berkeley, Calif.: Conari, 1999.

Levinson, Daniel J. *The Seasons of a Man's Life*. New York: Ballantine Books, 1978.

Marrs, Donald. *Executive in Passage*. Los Angeles: Barrington Sky Publishing, 1990.

May, Rollo. *Freedom and Destiny*. New York: W. W. Norton, 1981.

Merton, Thomas. *The Way of Chuang Tzu*. Boston: Shambhala, 1992.

Metzger, Bruce M. and Roland E. Murphy. *The New Oxford Annotated Bible*. New York: Oxford University Press, 1991.

Osterberg, Rolf. *Corporate Renaissance*. Novato, Calif.: Nataraj Publishing, 1993.

Phillips, Dorothy Berkley. *The Choice is Always Ours*. New York: Family Library, 1974.

Senge, Peter. *The Fifth Discipline*. New York: Doubleday, 1990.

Shak, Idries. *Tales of the Dervishes*. New York: E. P. Dutton, 1970.

Shield, Benjamin and Richard Carlson, Ph.D. *For the Love of God: New Writings By Spiritual and Psychological Leaders*. Novato, Calif.: New World Library, 1990.

Stone, Hal, Ph.D. and Sidra Winkelman, Ph.D. *Embracing Ourselves*. Novato, Calif.: New World Library, 1989.

Telushkin, Joseph. *Jewish Wisdom*. New York: William Morrow, 1994.

Thompson, Marjorie J. *Soul Feast*. Louisville, KY: Westminster/John Knox, 1995.

Thurman, Howard. *Disciplines of the Spirit*. Richmond, IN: Friends United Press, 1963.

Ueland, Brenda. *If You Want to Write: A Book About Art, Independence and Spirit*. Saint Paul, Minn.: Graywolf Press, 1987.

Underhill, Evelyn. *Practical Mysticism*. New York: E. P. Dutton and Company, 1915.

Walker, Barbara G. *The Crone: Woman of Age, Wisdom and Power*. New York: Harper Collins, 1985.

Wilhelm, Richard (translator) and Cary F. Baynes. *The I Ching*. Forward by Carl Jung. Princeton, NJ: Princeton University Press, 1950.

Index

The Journey to Inner Excellence Continues

For self-guided lessons, a monthly newsletter, consultations, news of my talks and workshops and more, please consult the Inner Excellence Web site at www.innerexcellence.com.